Kything

Kything
The Art
of Spiritual Presence

Louis M. Savary and
Patricia H. Berne

PAULIST PRESS
New York and Mahwah, N.J.

Calligraphy by Noreen Monroe Guzie.

Copyright © 1988 by Louis M. Savary and Patricia H. Berne

Library of Congress Cataloging-in-Publication Data

Savary, Louis M.
    Kything : the art of spiritual presence / by Louis M. Savary and Patricia
H. Berne.
      p.   cm.
    Includes bibliographies.
    ISBN 0-8091-3011-4 (pbk.) : $9.95 (est.)
     1. Spiritual life—Catholic authors. I. Berne, Patricia H.
II. Title.
BX2350.2.S266 1988
248—dc19   88-21783
                                          CIP

Published by Paulist Press
997 Macarthur Boulevard
Mahwah, N.J. 07430

Printed and bound in the
United States of America

Contents

Contents

KYTHING AND THE PSYCHOLOGICAL

Contents

KYTHING AND THE SPIRITUAL

KYTHING AND THE SACRED

Dedication
To Madeleine L'Engle
for giving a name to Kything;
to Suzanne, Eve, and Serena
Berne for giving life to it

Preface

There is a spiritual revolution going on in the world today. It has been gestating for at least half a century. Many claim it was spawned by a French scientist-priest Pierre Teilhard de Chardin who called for a revolutionary "conspiracy of love."

We usually think of a conspiracy as an attempt to overthrow a government. But at its roots "to conspire" means "to join spirits" or "to breathe together." Teilhard de Chardin's conspiracy is about getting millions of people to be lovingly joined at the level of spirit for the transformation of the world.

In 1980, Marilyn Ferguson became a kind of spokesperson for this revolutionary conspiracy called for by Teilhard de Chardin. Reporting in her book *The Aquarian Conspiracy* some of its already-achieved results, she described the many levels of social and spiritual transformation resulting from millions of individual personal transformations. These individual comrades in a leaderless but powerful network were spontaneously uniting, as conspirators for the sake of the earth, to bring about a cultural realignment in history.

Almost always throughout history people have tried to remake society by changing its outward form and organization. The conspiracy of love works differently. The spiritual conspirators individually undergo shifts that enable them to find germinating within themselves seeds of inner strength and a larger wisdom. They in turn plant this hope of a broader awakening into the furrows of society.

The both of us recognized ourselves as members of this conspiracy.

1

For years we have been planting our seeds in the books we wrote and the workshops we led on meditation-with-music, building self-esteem and spiritual growth, working with dreams to release human potential, applying creative energies to everyday living, designing holistic prayer forms, and defining spirituality. In each of these areas we followed the principle that by creating shifts of perspective in enough individuals a larger social paradigm shift would naturally occur.

This book marks a major movement in the tradition of spiritual practices designed to release spiritual energies in people and relationships. Kything, a new term for a familiar experience to some, provides an elementary tool for a technology of loving, spirit-to-spirit presence. To kythe (rhymes with "tithe" and "scythe") is an active verb describing an interactive spiritual process.

Just as kything is a tool for a spiritual technology, it is also the name for a spiritual art. While technology refers to skills you can be taught to do by others, art refers to the way those skills get expressed through your own unique personality. In this sense, art goes beyond technology.

We subtitled our book *The Art of Spiritual Presence* because the art of kything provides a personal outlet for very special energies; it taps into spiritual resources which have always been a part of you, waiting for expression. Any art allows you to make a unique, creative expression of yourself and what is most important to you. Kything is an art that allows you to put your personal stamp on things that are spiritually most important to you and to your relationships.

Many of us say we believe in a spiritual world but often we find ourselves denying it or avoiding it. Unconsciously we fight against the complexity that would come into our lives if we really believed in it and acted accordingly. We're used to living in the physical and mental worlds and explaining events in material and psychological terms, avoiding anything that might disturb the equilibrium of our ordinary lives. Almost nothing in the supermarket, the office or the home reminds us that there are other realms of existence that we need to explore if we are to become fully human and fully alive.

No matter how hard you try to deny it, your life is filled with spiritual events and you live immersed in the spiritual world. Your spirit continually calls for expression in some of the following ways: You find yourself wanting to create something beautiful—a poem, a song, a painting, a meal, a party, a garden, a relationship, a family, etc. You want to feel good about yourself, to feel a sense of self-esteem. You have felt the call to forgiveness and the urge to bring resolution to unsettled relationships. You long to show compassion, to love unconditionally. You know you have the power to heal. You want to make commitments and to fill your life with meaning and purpose. You seek wisdom. You struggle to find meaning in the events of your life. Your soul longs for deep friendships, and for union with God. All of these are spiritual activities and utilize your spiritual energies.

Some people never attempt to understand this spiritual world and use its dynamics. They seldom call upon their powers of courage, creativity, compassion, decisiveness, discernment. Many simply keep their spiritual eyes closed and never see what is going on in their own human spirit or that of others. Even though people may talk about the spiritual world, many of us do not reflect it in our behavior. As one old sage remarked to a person seeking spiritual growth: "If you believe that God exists, act as if you believe it."

As teachers we believe that people often fail to develop their human spirit, not because they don't want to grow spiritually, *but because they simply don't know how to help themselves grow.* For many, spiritual growth is not a problem of intention but of technology. In response to this problem we see ourselves as technicians of this spiritual realm and our task to develop tools and techniques for spiritual growth. To us kything is a most powerful basic spiritual skill, offering a way for members of the conspiracy of love to be *consciously* joined to each other, spirit-to-spirit.

In this book we hope to lead you, through kything, to create and explore the spiritual world that surrounds you.

Louis M. Savary, S.T.D., Ph.D.
Patricia H. Berne, Ph.D.
Washington, D.C.

Acknowledgements

In compiling a list of the people we wanted to thank for helping this book become a reality, we thought of hundreds of names. We can't print our appreciation list here for lack of space. But we do want to mention, at least collectively, all our hundreds of workshop participants and graduate students, especially those from St. Joseph College in West Hartford, who for the past decade have given us written feedback about their kything experiences, many of which are recorded in these pages.

Special thanks go to Mabel Murray and Martha Thompson who first encouraged Louis to explore Madeleine L'Engle's writings and to Patty Olert who gave him his first copy of *A Wind in the Door*.

The Basics of
Kything

1. What Is Kything?

Spiritual Presence

Kything may be most simply described as a *conscious act of spiritual presence.* Its primary purposes are to help deepen your relationships and help you live up to your own best potential.

What does it mean to be spiritually present to someone?

We often experience spiritual presence but seldom know how to name it. Here are three stories that involve spiritual presence.

Viktor Frankl, psychiatrist and author of *Man's Search for Meaning,* was one of the few who survived a World War II concentration camp. He was sustained, he said, by the loving connection he felt with his wife throughout his internment. Though the pair were separated physically, they continued to maintain a spiritual presence. Here is a description of the way kything happened one morning.

As my friend and I stumbled on for miles, slipping on icy spots, supporting each other time and time again, dragging one another up and onward, nothing was said but we both knew: each of us was thinking of his wife. Occasionally I looked at the sky, where the stars were fading and the pink light of the morning was beginning to spread behind a dark bank of clouds. But my mind clung to my wife's image, imagining it with an uncanny acuteness. I heard her answering me, saw her smile, her frank and encouraging look. Real or not, her look was then more luminous than the sun which was beginning to rise.[1]

In that moment, Frankl explained, he understood how a man who has nothing left in this world still may know bliss in the spiritual presence of his beloved. Even though Frankl could not express his concentration-camp life in positive achievements he could endure his sufferings in an honorable way and, "through loving contemplation of the image he carries of his beloved, achieve fulfillment."

The second story of spiritual presence is told by a mother about her ten-year-old daughter:

> When Suzy was in the fifth grade at a new school, she was kicked while playing a game in the schoolyard. Not wanting anyone to see her cry, she ran into the Girls' Room and "talked" to me. She said she sensed my presence, heard me talking to her, and felt me comforting her. After that, she was able to go back to the playground and re-enter the game. Later at home, when she was describing my presence to her in the Girls' Room, it was clear to her that the experience was different from a wish or a make-believe game, "I couldn't see you, mommy," she said, "but I could feel you there."

Suzy could clearly distinguish between physical presence, spiritual presence and imaginary presence (playing fantasy games).

The third example occurs in a story about a boy and his grandfather told to us by a friend of the boy.

> Josh who had been very close to his grandfather kept his grandfather's cap after the old man died. Often when Josh was having

---

[1] Viktor Frankl, *Man's Search for Meaning.* Boston: Beacon Press, 1959, p. 68.

a difficult time or was scared, he would take his grandfather's cap from the bureau and put it on his head. The grandfather also had a favorite easy chair in which Josh would sit whenever he wanted or felt he needed certain qualities—wisdom, comforting, guidance, valuing, patience—which his grandfather had often given him when he was alive. As far as Josh was concerned, even though the old man was no longer physically around, his grandfather's presence was still very much alive in the world and was capable of influencing him. The hat and the favorite chair were objects that made it easy for Josh to consciously enjoy that spiritual presence. Once, when Josh's mother wanted him to tell a lie, he refused, adding, "Grandfather would not want me to do a thing like that."

Without a doubt the boy still felt spiritually connected to his grandfather and at times like this called upon his grandfather's presence in order to live up to his own best potential.

People like Viktor Frankl and his wife, Suzy and her mother, Josh and his grandfather live and relate on at least three levels: physical, psychological, and spiritual. As persons, we are capable of being present to one another on each or all of these levels.

Physical Presence and Touching

Everyone knows what it means to be *physically present* to someone, for example, when you and I are standing in the same room, sitting in the same car or dancing together. When Josh's grandfather was still alive, he and Josh enjoyed each other's physical presence whenever they sat together, walked together or went fishing together. Suzy's mother often brushed her hair, rubbed her back, and helped her get dressed for school. The ways we experience body-to-body presence are by seeing, hearing, and touching one another, or by speaking and moving so that we are seen, heard, and felt.

The most general terms that describe the basic art of body-to-body presence are *movement* and *touching*. Techniques that may be used to enhance the quality of physical presence include seeing, dancing, shaking hands, hugging, kissing, physical coordination, body language, massage, and so on.

Psychological Presence and Communication

Everyone also knows what it means to be *psychologically* (emotionally or mentally) *present* to another, for example, when you and I are listening and talking to each other. Psychological presence is distinguishable from physical presence, since you and I can be together in the same room (physical presence) while our minds and thoughts (psychological presence) may be miles apart. When Josh's grandfather had been alive, he and Josh were often psychologically present to each other when they talked together, laughed, and shared stories. Suzy and her mother were psychologically present when Suzy telephoned her from a girlfriend's home or when her mother listened to Suzy talk about her classmates and important events as she drove her to and from school.

The most general term that describes the basic art of mind-to-mind presence is *communication*. The art of communication may be used to develop or improve psychological presence. Communication techniques include the skills of grammar, languages, conversation, active listening, letter-writing, reading, studying, teaching, counseling, rhetoric, commercial drawing, journalism, and many more.

Spiritual Presence and Communion

Is there a third kind of presence that is beyond physical and mental presence? Something distinguishable from body-to-body and mind-to-mind presence? Is there such a thing as soul-to-soul or *spirit-to-spirit pres-*

ence among humans? Logically, it would seem so. If we humans can operate on physical, mental, and spiritual levels, why would we not be able to be present to each other spirit-to-spirit?

Frankl clung to his wife's image, "imagining it with uncanny acuteness." So powerfully present was she despite her physical absence that Frankl struggled to define the "reality" of that powerful presence. Even while his mind was trying to make logical sense of the experience, Frankl knew without a doubt how real that spirit-to-spirit presence was: "I heard her answering me, saw her smile, her frank encouraging look." And if only for that brief moment, he knew bliss "in the contemplation of his beloved."

The most general word that describes the basic art of spirit-to-spirit presence is *communion.* It seems that Josh and his grandfather had found ways to be spiritually present to each other while the old man was still alive because Josh was able to re-establish this communion even after his death. Suzy was aware that though her mother wasn't physically present her essence was with her in the Girls' Room, and her mothering qualities were experienced by Suzy as a comforting presence.

Are there communion techniques and skills available (comparable to the many communication skills and techniques available) that people can learn in order to develop their ability to be spiritually present to others? We believe there are.

Three Levels of Human Activity

In this book we present kything as a very basic communion skill that can be used to establish spiritual presence between persons. The following schema distinguishes the three levels of human activity according to their kinds of presence and some of the arts and skills for establishing each kind of presence.

LEVEL OF HUMAN ACTIVITY	MODE OF PRESENCE	THE BASIC ART	TECHNIQUES/ SKILLS
Physical	Body-to-Body	Movement, Touching	Seeing, touching, hearing, moving, dancing, hugging, etc.
Psychological	Mind-to-Mind	Communication	Active listening, writing, talking, counseling, etc.
Spiritual	Spirit-to-Spirit	Communion	Kything, prayer, meditation, sacramental communion, etc.

Spiritual Presence Among Friends

From time immemorial, holy and religious people have believed that spiritual presence is not only possible but also quite normal among friends.

St. Gregory the Great and many of the early Christian leaders and teachers were conscious of their spiritual presence to each other. For them, friendship was the medium of this presence. "Friendship is a union of souls and a joining of hearts," Gregory wrote to his friend Theotimus in the sixth century. "Friends are *cor unum et anima una* (one heart and one soul). As the love of God (*caritas*) is the custodian of virtue, so is my friend the custodian of my soul."

Gregory wrote that he and Theotimus were "of one soul," so much so that they need never be separated in spirit even when they were absent in body. Such spiritual union may include others as well, for Gregory ends his letter with a request for a friend whom he knows Theotimus "loves with the same love you have for me."

Two centuries before, in a letter to his dear friend St. Basil the Great, St. Gregory Nazianzus wrote in a similar vein: "It seems as though there were but one soul between us, having two bodies. And if we must not believe those who say that all things are in all things [a pantheistic theory heretical to Christian thought], yet you must believe this, that we are both in each one of us, and the one in the other. . . . "

During the sixteenth century, the famous St. Teresa of Avila was a very close friend of Peter of Alcantara who frequently came to her in spiritual presence, much as Viktor Frankl's wife came to him. Teresa called these spiritual visits "appearances." In the *Autobiography of St. Teresa of Avila,* she wrote:

> One of his appearances to me took place a year before his death.
> I was away at the time; and, knowing he was soon to die, I told
> him so, when he was some leagues from here. When he expired
> there, he appeared to me here and said that he was going to rest.
> I did not believe this, but repeated the story to a number of people
> and in a week came the news that he was dead—or, to put it bet-
> ter, that he had entered upon eternal life.[2]

Teresa's contact with Peter did not diminish after his death but rather increased. Through their spiritual presence she grew in wisdom, and together they were able to make a difference in people's lives.

> Since Peter's death it has been the Lord's good pleasure that I
> should have more interaction with him than I had during his life
> and that he should advise me on many subjects. I have often be-
> held him enjoying the greatest bliss. The first time he appeared to
> me he remarked on the blessedness of the penance that had won
> him so great a prize, and he spoke of many other things as well. . . .
> He is a much greater comfort to me, I think, than when he was on
> earth. . . . Many things which I have commended to him so that he
> should ask the Lord for them I have seen granted.[3]

---

[2]*Autobiography of St. Teresa of Avila,* trans. E. Allison Peers. New York: Doubleday, 1960, p. 257.

[3]*Ibid.,* pp. 251–58.

Teresa was conscious that Peter's "appearances" were of a spiritual nature and were happening through the imagination, not through the external senses: "Although this vision is imaginary," she wrote, "I never saw it, or any other vision, with the eyes of the body, but only with the eyes of the soul."[4]

Through the centuries friendship enabled these holy people and many others to discover and utilize their ability to commune with each other as well as communicate. As the stories of Viktor Frankl, Suzy, and Josh attest, that same spiritual ability is available to us today to discover and utilize.

---

[4]*Ibid.,* p. 258.

2. How Kything Got Its Name

The First Appearance of "Kything"

The name kything was first used by Madeleine L'Engle to describe a spiritual technique in her novel *A Wind in the Door.* In the story, Proginoskes is a pure-spirit, angelic cherubim who sometimes spurts fire; Meg is an American adolescent girl.

> Proginoskes looked at her with two, ringed owl-like eyes. "You're beginning to learn how to kythe."
>
> "To what?"
>
> "Kythe. It's how cherubim talk. It's talking without words, just the same way that I can be myself and not be enfleshed."
>
> "But I have to be enfleshed, and I need words."
>
> "I know, Meg," he replied gently, "and I will keep things worded for you. But it will help if you will remember that cherubim kythe without words among each other. For a human creature you show a distinct talent for kything."
>
> She blushed slightly at the compliment. . . . [1]

Not only did Meg have a distinct talent for kything, but most people also have a natural talent for it and can develop the skill as Meg did.

As the story progresses, Meg learns to kythe well in relating to the cherubim. She begins to recognize kything as a means of spirit-to-spirit

---

[1] Madeleine L'Engle, *A Wind in the Door.* New York: Dell, 1973, p. 88.

presence and also as a way to communicate within that presence. However, since thinking and talking out loud are so natural to her, the cherubim Proginoskes has to remind her from time to time simply to kythe.

> She hit the clenched fist of one hand against the palm of the other. "Wait. You told me to think, and I'm thinking."
> "You don't have to think out loud. You don't have to talk to think, after all. You're deafening me. Try to kythe with me, Meg."
> "I still don't understand kything. Is it like mental telepathy?"
> Proginoskes hesitated. "You might say that mental telepathy is the very beginning of learning how to kythe. But the cherubic language is entirely kything—with you, with stars, with galaxies, with the salt in the ocean, the leaves of the trees."
> "But I'm not a cherubim. How do I do it?"
> "Meg, your brain stores all the sensory impressions it receives, but your conscious mind doesn't have a key to the storehouse. All I want you to do is open yourself up to me so that I can open the door to your mind's storehouse."
> "All right, I'll try." To open herself entirely to the cherubim, to make herself completely vulnerable, was not going to be easy. But she trusted Proginoskes implicitly.[2]

Kything. The word in that book was fascinating, the concept intriguing, its implications enormous. Could the word and the concept offer a key to a method of establishing spiritual presence among humans, just as Madeline L'Engle imagined it doing among the angelic spirits and between them and Meg?

It seemed unusual to expect that a concept developed in a science fiction story marketed originally for young people would plant the seeds of a spiritual practice that could revolutionize spirituality. However, Madeleine L'Engle was also a very deeply spiritual and wise woman, an author of many books on spirituality for adults. How natural that her new ideas

---

[2] *Ibid.,* p. 96.

in spirituality would overflow into her "spiritual" fiction for young people. With the concept of kything she was tapping into a spiritual truth that she knew and recognized was, at some level, a familiar experience for many spiritual people.

From Concept to Technique

A year after *A Wind in the Door* was published, some friends of ours at a workshop introduced us to the book. We began exploring the idea of kything and developing techniques for using it. As we shared these techniques we gathered more information and techniques, and began to develop the art of kything. We recognized some of the far-reaching implications of the kything concept for spirituality and refined its definition as "spirit-to-spirit presence," even though its effects touched the physical and psychological dimensions as well. In workshops we suggested how and when people might commune, as Proginoskes observed, with people, angels, animals, trees, plants, galaxies, and even God. Workshop participants responded enthusiastically and shared their kything experiences with us.

One woman said, "A major gift of the weekend came through learning to kythe. I left the workshop with a strong feeling of oneness with all creation. On the way home I was waiting for a traffic light to change. I noticed a red tulip. I kythed with it and so with all creation."

Where Does the Word "Kything" Come From?

In 1977, we wrote to Madeleine L'Engle to ask about the etymology of kything. She wrote back: "While I was writing *A Wind in the Door* I spent a long time finding the word I needed, and finally came across kythe in *Jamieson's Scottish Dictionary,* published in 1856, which I inherited from my grandfather. The first definition is 'to be manifest'; the second, 'to come in sight'; the third, 'to appear in proper character' and he quotes, 'he will kythe in his ain colours' with the explanation added, 'he will appear without disguise.'"

If you have a comprehensively large English dictionary, you might find an entry under the spelling "kithe" or "kythe." It's an old Scottish word, as Madeleine L'Engle said, derived from the same root as the familiar words "kith" and "kin." Among the definitions found there will probably be something like "to show yourself in your own true guise" or "to show yourself without any disguise or mask." That's the way your kith and kin know you. That's the way Viktor Frankl's wife showed herself to him, and that's the way Peter of Alcantara showed himself to St. Teresa of Avila.

For our purpose, we might define the verb "kythe" as "to present your soul to another" or "to make your spirit manifest to another" or "to show your true Self to another." Madeleine L'Engle used the word in much the same sense as we do, as a conscious act of spiritual presence.

Jean Houston, also inspired by the kything concept in *A Wind in the Door,* teaches her workshop participants how to kythe. She describes kything as "deep resonance" or "deep flowing together" and "common thinking."

Generically, we call kything an act of spiritual presence. To be "in kythe" is consciously to have made your spirit manifest to another in a spiritual relationship. Cherubim, who are angels, must kythe because they are pure spirits. *Humans may kythe because we have a spiritual dimension.*

The Importance of a Name

Many people in our classes and workshops tell us they have been kything for years, except they never had a word to describe their experience. As one woman said, "Kything and the practice of spiritual presence was a real joy to experience. I have been doing this for a long time but never knew it had a name." How very fortunate that Madeleine L'Engle gave kything its name. When a concept has a name, you can begin exploring and working with it.

As technicians of the spiritual, we know that having a name is important. When a spiritual process or practice is without a name or a definition, people can never be sure they are talking about the same experience. Truck drivers who use CB radios to communicate with each other refer to a driver's name as a "handle" and they will often ask a new driver, "What's your handle?" Once you have named and defined a spiritual practice, you have a handle on it, and you can begin to study, test, and research it to see if it proves to be a useful and effective tool for spiritual growth.

In the past ten years we have explored many avenues of kything. Having a name for it has enabled us to develop many ways to use it.

Others Who Describe Spiritual Presence

It was important to explore different ideas about spiritual presence wherever we found them and relate them to kything. The most frequent finds were in novels.

For example, in *Timeless,* a novel written by the Russian Prince Nicholas Tchkotova in 1949, the main character in the story describes a spirit-to-spirit presence he enjoyed with his beloved Taya.

Mademoiselle Agathe was not very sensitive, but even she felt that something was going on between Taya and me. What puzzled her was that we made no attempt to be alone and that our conversation was totally free from any amorous implications. What she could not understand was that we did not need any outward display to know each other's heart, we were always alone with our love, even in the midst of the crowd. Our spiritual and mental nearness, the sense of oneness, was far more precious to us than all the words of love we could possibly express in any language.[3]

We also noticed acts of spiritual presence similar to kything described in other popular fiction, for example, in Alexandre Dumas' *The Corsican Brothers,* Emily Bronte's *Wuthering Heights,* Frank Herbert's *The Dosadi Experiment,* Robert Heinlein's *Stranger in a Strange Land,* and Richard Bach's

---

[3]Prince Nicholas Tchkotova, *Timeless.* Culver City, CA: Murray & Gee, Inc., 1949, pp. 55–56.

The Bridge Across Forever. As far as we can tell, kything as a spiritual practice between people is described (though not named as kything) with
some frequency in novels and poetry, but it has never been discussed or
given a clear name in the literature of spirituality.

Another fascinating example of spiritual presence is described in a
poem that came from the Cherokee Indian Reservation in North Carolina
in 1891, which is titled "Formula to Attract Affections." It is in fact consid-
ered to be a love charm to be recited by the lover to his beloved. We quote
here only the few lines of a very long piece that mention spirit-to-spirit
presence:

> No one is ever lonely with me. I am handsome.
> Let her put her soul into the very center of my soul,
> Never to turn away.
> Grant that in the midst of men
> She shall never think of them . . .
> No one is ever lonely with me.
> Your soul has come into the very center of my soul,
> Never to turn away.[4]

"Spiritual Intuition" and "Participatory Consciousness"

We researched others who talked about spiritual presence using other
language, and found certain similarities as well as differences.

For some, "spiritual intuition" is similar to kything. In an article in the
Journal of Transpersonal Psychology, transpersonal psychologist Frances
Clark reported on Robert Gerard's four levels of intuition corresponding to
the physical, emotional, mental, and spiritual levels of consciousness. She
explained how Gerard differentiates mental intuition from spiritual intuition.

> On a mental level, intuition operates as an irrational factor in prob-
> lem solving, as when the solution is reached suddenly by a leap

---

[4]This poem may be found in its entirety in *American Indian Prose and Poetry: An An-
thology,* Margot Astrov, ed. New York: Capricorn Books, 1962.

of imagination, rather than as a result of deductive reasoning. *Intuition on a spiritual level enables one to tune in on the inner core of being of another person, transcending the external aspects of the personality.* This level of intuition may be cultivated by an attitude of loving acceptance, a suspension of judgment, and non-analytic, empathetic understanding.[5]

In Robert Gerard's language kything employs the faculty of spiritual intuition, which enables you to be present to ("to tune in on") another's spirit ("inner core of being of another person"). Like kything, intuitive tuning in on the inner core of another is a spiritual event which transcends the external aspects of personality. In other words, when you kythe you are in touch with the spirit or soul of another in a way that can go beyond being present to their body, emotions, mind, or ordinary external events that are happening at the time of the kything. According to Gerard, it would be your spiritual intuition that establishes the kythe. In this book, we simply say it is you or your spirit that kythes.

Another concept that resonates well with kything is called "participatory consciousness." It was described by Beatrice Bruteau in *Anima* magazine. When you are in the presence of another person, your mind and your senses tend to grasp elements and details of the other person, but your spirit ("one's own centered, subjective being") can grasp the totality or essence of the person.

It grasps what it understands as a whole, as a real concrete being, immediately, as a unique instance or self, not as a member of a class or in terms of its categorizable attributes.[6]

---

[5]Frances Clark, "Exploring Intuition: Prospects and Possibilities," *Journal of Transpersonal Psychology,* vol. 2, 1973, p. 161 (italics added).

[6]Beatrice Bruteau, "Neo-Feminism and the Next Revolution in Consciousness," *Anima,* Spring 1977. The same article was reprinted in the Summer 1977 issue of *Cross Currents* (pp. 170–182).

When acting in participatory consciousness, explained Bruteau, you are actively centered in your own subjective being, and have also entered into the subject-being of another. In this sense, it is like kything. However, participatory consciousness, like any "consciousness," involves a way of looking at the world. Here is the way Bruteau describes the worldview of participatory consciousness: "I see that what the other is *is* some of my life energy living there, and what I am is some of the other's life energy living here in me. I can no longer divide the world into 'we's' and 'they's.' "

Kything would happen very naturally in participatory consciousness, but to be able to kythe does not demand that you assume the worldview of participatory consciousness, i.e., that the life energy of others is living in you and part of your life energy is living in others.

Beatrice Bruteau's ideas challenged us to begin developing a view of reality in which to situate the process of kything. We address this theme in the Appendix, "Where and When Does Kything Happen?"

Triangles

Triangles is the name of a service activity sponsored by the Lucis Trust. Its goal is to link men and women of good will in a worldwide spiritual service for the distribution of constructive spiritual energies. The process they use is a lot like kything.

A triangle is a group of three people who link each day for a few minutes in thought and meditation. The people need not live in the same locality since there are many international triangles.

Each day members sit quietly for a few minutes and link mentally with other members of their triangle, or triangles. [You can belong to more than one triangle.] They invoke the energies of light and goodwill, visualize these energies as circulating through the three focal points of each triangle, and pouring out through the network of triangles surrounding the planet. . . .

The work takes only a few minutes to perform and can be fitted into the most crowded program. It is not necessary for members to synchronize the time at which the work is done, as once a triangle is built and functioning, it can be vitalized by any one of its members.[7]

The network is built and maintained by the daily action of each triangle worker invoking spiritual energies and using the creative power of the mind. The motive of triangle workers is not primarily personal benefit, but to be at the service of the world's spiritual needs. The organization's goal is to raise the level of human consciousness and to transform the mental and spiritual climate of the planet.

The Technology of Kything

Our research into areas such as "triangles," "spiritual intuition," and "participatory consciousness" forced us to clarify our understanding of the word we had chosen and the process behind it. Although we do explore some of the philosophical foundations of kything, our primary interest is the technology of kything: how to carry it out successfully.

What we hope to do in this book is show people how to practice kything and develop it: how to handle the experience, explore its potentials, and integrate it into their other spiritual practices. As you can see from the work of the Triangles organization, kything has worldwide as well as personal implications.

As a skill, kything is able to fit into just about any religious or spiritual tradition and enrich it. Even if you don't think of yourself as belonging to a religious denomination or practicing a spiritual tradition, you can still use kything in your everyday life as Josh, Suzy, Viktor Frankl, Madeleine L'Engle, and many others have.

---

[7]For further information, write to Triangles, 866 United Nations Plaza, Suite 566–7, New York, NY 10164.

3. How Do I Kythe?

Three Essential Steps

If you want to kythe with God, another human, or anything else, there are three essential steps to the process:

> **(1) Get centered.**
> **(2) Focus on the other and**
> **(3) Establish connection or union.**

Step 1: Get Centered

Since kything is primarily a spiritual process, it is important at the outset that you be present to your own human spirit. The simplest and most sure way of doing this is to get centered. Centering, which is a holistic process, means quietly focusing the attention of your body, mind, and spirit on yourself. Suzy did this by going into one of the stalls of the Girls' Room and closing the door so she could be quiet and alone. Josh carried out this first step by sitting quietly in his grandfather's rocking chair. In a strange way, Viktor Frankl also got centered in his own body because walking silently on the icy, slippery terrain forced him to stay focused on himself.

As you gently and lovingly focus on yourself, your body begins to grow relaxed, your mind calm, and your spirit moves toward being peacefully at rest. When this centered state of consciousness takes over, you are "at home" in yourself. You are present to yourself and you can affirm, "I am present to myself: body, mind, and spirit."

The more you practice getting centered the easier it becomes and the more quickly you can become present to yourself. Eventually you will be able to center yourself in a few moments. For St. Ignatius Loyola the time it took to recite "The Lord's Prayer" was usually enough. In moments of crisis or intense feeling, as with Suzy, people report becoming centered almost instantly. Of course, in time of crisis it is also possible to panic and enter into a state of terror, which is quite the opposite of being centered. In terror you are "beside yourself," not within yourself.

When you are centered you are able to say, *"I am present to myself."*

By the way, to be centered does not mean to be sleepy or "spaced out." It means to have your whole self—body, mind, spirit—present and focused.

Techniques for Centering

There are a number of ways to get centered. Just about every Eastern and Western spiritual tradition proposes its own favorite ways of centering, such as: counting the breath, focusing on the breathing process, repeating a ritual movement, reciting sacred words, chanting, dancing, creating an imaginative scene, and so on. Kything does not require that you use any particular centering technique. Josh's favorite way was to put on his grandfather's cap and sit in his rocking chair. If you already have a favorite way to get centered, you will probably want to use it when kything. If not, here are a few simple techniques, all of which begin with the following preparatory steps:

To prepare for centering:

1. **Sit or lie down comfortably and close your eyes.**
2. **Slowly take a few deep breaths and let your body begin to grow quiet.**
3. **Give your mind and imagination something to focus on, so that they too begin to grow quiet. Here are a few simple techniques for doing this last step:**

25

Centering Technique 1: Begin by numbering each breath you take, say, from one to six; when you have counted six breaths, begin over again, numbering the next breath as "one." Continue numbering each breath you take, from one to six, for a few minutes or until your mind grows quiet. If you lose count at any time, simply begin counting again starting at "one."

Centering Technique 2: Focus your mind and imagination upon some part of your body involved in the breathing process, say, your nostrils. Then, as if you were a camera, simply pay attention to the breath as it passes your nostrils, going in and coming out. Keep focused there for a few minutes or until you begin to grow quiet. If you get distracted, simply refocus your attention to your nostrils and continue watching the breath going in and coming out.

Centering Technique 3: Say your name quietly each time you exhale. Do this for a few minutes or until you grow quiet. This procedure is called repeating a *mantra.* Mantra means "a sound that has spiritual power." In this technique you are using your name as a mantra. You could of course use any other name, word or phrase you like in order to get centered. Many people find using their own name works very effectively.

Dealing with Distractions

The objective of centering is to quiet your body, mind, and spirit so that your spirit can become the "center" of your attention. For, it is your spirit that kythes. Suzy found a quiet place in the Girls' Room and got comfortable there; she went inward instead of focusing on the sounds outside, her playmates or even her pain and anger. She didn't deny the reality of these distractions, she simply did not want them to be the center of her attention. Intuitively she knew that she should stay focused on her spirit and eventually on her mother's spiritual presence.

Usually the main hindrance to getting centered is that your body and mind are so busy and distracted that it is impossible for you to feel your spirit's presence. How do you deal with distractions?

When you want to get deeply centered, put aside whatever might be absorbing your sensory attention, for example, a television program, people moving about, conversation, noise outside your room, and so on. It is not impossible to kythe while watching television, walking down the street, standing in a room full of people or driving a car. Indeed, at times you may want to kythe with someone precisely to share the joy of these experiences. However, when getting centered you will be successful only to the degree that your attention is not captive to the sensory stimuli around you.

People may tell you that when you are centered you are not doing anything; usually they assert that being centered is a state of being, not a state of doing. This is true in the sense that you are not doing the kinds of things you normally do in your daily activities. It is also true in the sense that when you finally get centered you have reached a new state of consciousness. But *in the process of getting to that state* you are in fact doing things to quiet your body and mind. And sometimes you get distracted. Spiritual teachers have long known that it is unhelpful to tell humans *not* to do something. So, instead of telling you *not* to be distracted, good teachers tell you what to do when you are distracted. Usually their advice is: "Begin the centering process again." Doing this will quickly help you regain your focus of attention and re-establish your centered state.

Step 2: Focus on the Other

Once you are centered in yourself, you can shift your focus of attention from yourself to the person with whom you want to kythe. In this step you begin to "center" on the other person.

Suzy focused her attention on her mother. She probably pictured her in her imagination and may have repeated the special name she called her mother like a chant in her heart or quietly out loud. Josh probably did something similar.

This second step describes a special state of consciousness which we call being lovingly single-minded or *single-focused on an object.* It is a holistic state in which you hold your kything partner in a contemplative gaze. Viktor Frankl used this very word to describe this step as he experienced it; he said it happened "through loving contemplation of the image he carries of his beloved." Frankl had an image of his wife that he had probably recalled in his imagination thousands of times in his life. By now that image had attained a definition of "uncanny acuteness" and it was "more luminous than the sun."

In religious traditions such contemplation is a common spiritual practice. During contemplation you quietly and lovingly gaze at the object of your prayer or love, e.g., God or a beloved person. You might use a statue, a picture, a symbol, or simply form a mental image in order to focus your attention and hold it. Mothers often gaze at their children (or even photographs of their children) in a contemplative way. They can stay focused on the object of their love for long periods of time without much analytical thinking. A mother's gaze is holistic in that her body, mind, and spirit are all involved in being present to the child. People who value art and nature often gaze for long periods of time quietly and lovingly at a sculpture, a portrait, the ocean or a meadow. In this way they seem to penetrate to the level of spirit.

Use your imagination to become present to your kything partner. When this step is complete, you will be able to say, "I am present to you in spirit." At first, it usually takes a full minute or two to contemplatively focus on your kything partner. The more you practice being single-focused, the better you become at it and the more quickly you can complete this step of the kything process. People who kythe with their spouse each day soon learn to do all three steps in a minute.

When you are fully focused on your kything partner you can say, *"I am present to your spirit."*

Essential Steps

Step 1 and Step 2 are important because they assure you that you are doing kything with your whole self, not just with your mind. These two steps make the difference between just "thinking about" your partner and making a spirit-to-spirit connection. Thinking about and connecting are two very different actions. During an ordinary day, you often think about people and even have emotional reactions to them. You can do this without ever spiritually connecting with them or becoming present to them at the level of spirit. Perhaps Viktor Frankl's companion was also thinking of his wife, worrying about her, wondering if they would ever escape from the concentration camp and find each other again. Perhaps Frankl's companion never got beyond the stage of worrying and wondering about his wife to the stage of spiritually connecting with her. By getting in touch with your own center in Step 1 and by getting focused on your kything partner's spirit in Step 2, you prepare yourself for true spirit-to-spirit connection.

Techniques for Focusing on Your Kything Partner

Just as you have been focusing on your breathing, or counting, or using some image or word to help you relax and grow centered, you now begin focusing on the person with whom you will kythe. In this step you shift your attention to your kything partner. Here are some ways to do this:

Focusing Technique 1: If the person is physically present, you may quietly and lovingly gaze at him or her. There is no need to follow the other's movements or analyze what he or she is doing. Simply look at the other, because that is where his or her spirit is centered. Stay focused in this way until you can say, "I am present to your spirit."

Focusing Technique 2: If the person is not physically present, form a picture of the person in your imagination. As Frankl put it, "My mind clung to my wife's image." This image may focus on others' physical appearance or some part of them (face, hands, feet, eyes) or on them engaged in some typical physical activity (cooking, laughing, driving, painting, dancing, reading, sleeping). Josh probably held his grandfather's hat lovingly and stroked its brim, or perhaps he pictured his grandfather quietly rocking in the old rocker. Look at the image lovingly and peacefully until you can say, "I am present to your spirit."

Focusing Technique 3: If you want to kythe with someone but have no idea what the person looks like, hold in your imagination a picture of some identifying object or symbol associated with that person such as a hat, a chair, a book, the ocean. If you have no image or none spontaneously occurs, you may focus on the person's name, as Suzy probably did with her mother's name, "Mommy." For example, you can repeat it subvocally as a

29

mantra or visualize it written out or printed in your imagination. Use whatever procedure will help you focus on your kything partner until you can say, "I am present to your spirit."

If you get distracted or lose focus on your kything partner, simply let go of the distraction and return to focus. Some people think that if they get distracted they have somehow failed. The fact is that everyone gets distracted now and then, no matter how expert he or she may be. *Part of doing this second step is to return to focus whenever you become distracted.* The only time you fail is when you give up attempting to return to focus.

Step 3: Establish Connection

This third step is when communion happens, that is, when you and your kything partner form a union or a oneness. In this third step you establish a spirit-to-spirit connection between you and your partner, so that the two of you become joined freely and lovingly to each other at the level of spirit. Although kything is a very elementary spiritual act, it is an affirmation and an experience of a profound union.

When this step is complete you will be able to say, *"We are present spirit-to-spirit"* or *"We are in communion."*

Two Parts to Communion Step

How is this connection established? There are two parts to this communion step:

1. **Envision or symbolically image the two of you physically present to each other and forming a bond,** e.g., I picture you and me standing face-to-face smiling at each other.
2. **Make a choice to create what you envision, to make the union of you and the other a reality**, (an inner reality, but nonetheless a reality).

Your choice-making puts into motion whatever forces are needed to establish the spirit-to-spirit connection that you envision.

The Power of Choice

There is nothing mysterious about your power of choice. You use it every day. If there is a result you want, e.g., to buy a new suit, to write a letter, to sell something to a client, to have a serious talk with a family member about finances, etc., your *choice to create this result* puts into motion the forces that are needed to produce it. Nothing happens without your choice. Physical presence cannot happen unless you choose to meet me. Psychological presence cannot happen unless you choose to listen to me and to share. In the same way, the spiritual union you seek in kything cannot be created except through your choice.

As Rollo May pointed out, the words "I choose" and "I will" are expressions of your identity. "Our human task," he writes, "is to unite love and will. They are not united by biological growth but must be part of our conscious development." Choosing a result you want is a central experience of being human and a direct expression of who you are. Kything offers you the opportunity directly to unite your love and will, and to express who you are.

The Role of Imagery

The function of the imagery-making in the first part of this step is to provide a symbolic image of the object or result you want to choose. To establish the desired communion experience, create an image in your imagination of the two of you joined together. This imagery can take any form that satisfies your sense of oneness. For example, you can picture both of you surrounded by divine light. You may picture you and your partner eating from the same plate or sharing the same cup. You may picture the two of you kissing or hugging. You may imagine the two of you together in the same automobile, sitting together at the same cafe table, or walking hand-in-hand on a woodland path. You may choose to be more symbolic in your imagery and picture the two of you as two leafs on the same branch, two peas in a pod, two raindrops in the same puddle or two rolling waves in the same ocean. You may picture the other person's body inside your skin, or your body inside his or hers. If you wish to employ religious imagery, you may picture you and your partner held in the palm of God's hand or held together by a shimmering light of divine power. Use whatever image facilitates your choice to be one with your partner in spiritual presence.

One man we know likes to do this step by inviting his partner's spirit into his heart. He pictures his heart as a quiet cottage and both of them sit together inside the cottage. A woman likes to do this step by projecting her spirit to a place where she meets the spirit of her partner. At various times she envisions the meeting place as a clearing in the woods, a sunny meadow, a sacred building, a favorite vacation place, or somewhere in space. Once they are both there, they hold hands and kiss as symbols of communion.

Remember that the imagery in this step—whatever imagery you use—is simply the vehicle by which you enter the kything experience. The imagery is not the kythe. Such images represent an inner and not necessarily an outer reality. Nor is any particular image essential, since theoretically you can kythe without imagery, perhaps through strong affect or sensory clues. Nevertheless, we tend to agree with Aristotle who in his treatise *On the Soul* observed that "the soul never thinks without an image."

In kything, image and choice work together. Although choice or will is essential in establishing the connection, the power of effective imagery can never be overestimated. As Emile Coue once observed, "When the will and the imagination are in conflict, it is always the imagination that wins." For this reason, the imagery you use to envision the communion can often help deepen and prolong the kythe.

Ending a Kythe

Just as a kythe may be initiated by your personal choice, so it may be ended in the same manner. You may withdraw your spiritual presence by choosing to do so or by focusing your spiritual presence somewhere else. You can put an end to *physical* presence by walking away, getting out of the car, getting up from the table, closing a door behind you, etc. You may stop *psychological* presence by turning your mind's attention to something else, for example, hanging up the telephone, turning to another person, picking up your pen to write a letter, and so on. In a similar way you can bring a kythe to an end by choosing to remove your *spiritual* presence. You might do this mentally by envisioning yourself walking away from the communion scene and choosing to break the spirit-to-spirit connection. You may also make a break in the spiritual connection by doing something physical. Suzy did it by going back out to the playground. Josh probably did it by getting up from the rocker and doing his homework. Viktor Frankl would have been brought out of his kythe when his companion spoke to him.

Of course, by your choice you may re-establish the kythe whenever you want. Frankl probably re-entered the kythe with his wife as soon as he and his companion stopped talking. A summary of the three steps in kything:

1. **Center:** "I am present to myself."
2. **Focus:** "I am present to your spirit."
3. **Connect:** "We are present spirit-to-spirit."

4. How Should I Practice Kything?

Take Time To Practice Kything

Usually, at this point in workshops we ask people to try kything with someone. So, think of someone with whom you would like to kythe. To start, choose someone you love and who loves you. It may be a member of your family or a dear friend. It makes no difference whether that person is near or far, physically present or absent. Let it be someone you think would agree to enter into spiritual union with you for a few minutes. Once you have selected a kything partner, follow the three steps described above: (1) get centered, (2) focus on your partner, and (3) establish a connection.

During her first year away at college, Jane who had been in therapy at home for the past year would sometimes feel a need to think things through and so would write a letter to her therapist. Before beginning to write, she would grow quiet, focus on her therapist in her imagination, and begin to formulate her first sentence. As she wrote each statement she would begin thinking about the kind of response her therapist might make to it. When she finished her letter she might mail it or not, because in the process she had received the help and direction she had been seeking. She began to enjoy this kind of spiritual connection and frequently utilized letter-writing to her therapist for inner support. When Jane described these experiences to her therapist at a visit during the holidays, the therapist acknowledged that the "help and direction" Jane had received during those times of spiritual presence were exactly what she would have recommended. "What Jane 'heard' me say or imagined me saying during those moments was me at my best," acknowledged the therapist.

34

Jane hadn't known the name for kything then, but she was doing it naturally. Now that she knows the proper steps for achieving spirit-to-spirit presence, she does so with confidence in many different ways with many different people.

Today, some years later, Jane and her partner are often in different cities on weekends leading workshops. They agree to kythe with each other at a certain hour each day; for them, those few minutes, which they remind themselves of with a wrist alarm, are a very special time of their day when they are joined in spirit and know that they live in a mutual love.

If you spend some time practicing kything now, especially if you have never done it before, you will gain two obvious benefits. First, by experiencing kything you will know what we're talking about and be able to read the rest of the book from the point of view of someone who has been there. Second, every bit of practice you do improves your kything skill.

Kything in Families

One of the most natural contexts for kything is in the family. Kything can promote love, sincerity, and openness for children and the family as a whole.

Teach children about kything so they can know how to do it at an early age and take advantage of it for the rest of their lives. Most children spontaneously know how to kythe or can learn the steps for it by the age of four. Children are helped by having a name for this process. Then, with a little encouragement and an invitation, most will gladly kythe with you. And when they need your spiritual support, they will initiate the communion.

In introducing kything to her young child, Terri began by telling four-year-old Angela, "Go quiet inside yourself. Say your name quietly over and over and see how it takes you into your heart and soul, and tell me when you are there. I will go into my soul at the same time." When Angela reported that she was in her heart her mother said, "Okay. Now, let your soul creep over to mine—or slide over, if you like. Then when we are together in my soul we can slide back over together to you."

Terri was describing to her daughter in simple language the three

35

steps of kything: how to get centered, how to focus on another's spirit, and how to establish a spirit-to-spirit connection.

Kythe with children as they say their night prayers, or explicitly make kything a standard part of their night prayers. Teach them to kythe with God and the saints as well as with each of the persons for whom they pray or ask God to bless.

When children are asleep, many parents before bed take a moment to pop into the child's room only to adjust the covers and leave. Such parents could also pause a few moments for a loving kythe. During the kythe, they could speak to the child's soul some affirming and loving words that would build the child's self-confidence and self-esteem at the deepest levels.

One mother we knew described how she used to speak spontaneously to her child's soul:

> I often wondered how my daughter maintained her self-confidence and healthy self-esteem after growing up with so much criticism from her father. Then I remembered how, for years when she was very young, I used to go into her room when she was asleep, gaze lovingly at her and say aloud but very softly, "I love you." Invariably my daughter would smile in her sleep and reply softly, "I know." It was as if her spirit answered me and never forgot that she was lovable and loved.

A child who learns to kythe and develops skill creating spirit-to-spirit presence can grow into an adult very sensitively tuned into spiritual realities.

Invite children to kythe with you when they go off to school. Instead of just kissing them goodbye, consciously kythe with them as you kiss them or touch them. Let them kythe with you too. Teach them that they can reaffirm a spiritual connection with you whenever they want. By kything, they can quickly share important things with you—joy, loneliness, success, or when they feel sick and are not sure what they should do.

It is important to note that kything is not to be used to prevent the natural, healthy process of individuation and separation that all children must gradually make from their parents. Rather, kything is designed as a supportive reality that smooths the process of separation and nurtures a healthy sense of self-valuing in the child. Instead of unhealthy dependence, its two-way nature encourages a healthy sense of interdependence.

Kythe with children during a fearful time, and remind them they can kythe with you whenever they are anxious or afraid. As an adult you can consciously establish a spiritual bond with individual family members and choose to maintain that connection as you go about your daily activities. There is no need to stay consciously focused on the communion, since you and the other person can return to it whenever you want by kything.

During your own personal prayer time kythe with family members and see them standing before you surrounded by a circle of holy light. If you are a Christian, acknowledge and affirm that Christ is alive and full of purpose in each one with whom you kythe. In this way you develop a deep reverence for each member of your family and for your family as a whole.

When you come together for a meal, instead of simply reciting Grace Before Meals, take a few moments to kythe with each member and with the family as a unique unit of love in the world. To let the experience be savored and expressed, ask family members to say what it feels like to be spiritually connected to each of the others.

Kythe also before an important family discussion, so that you are resolving problems from within a state of communion. You can do this even though you may mentally disagree with or are emotionally angry at each other.

Kything for Married Couples

Couples may use kything as a grounding for their marriage and a foundation for building a deep spiritual union. Couples can pray in kythe. At the beginning of your shared prayer or meditation period consciously kythe with each other. In this way you perform your spiritual practices from within your loving union.

Bill and Alice take a walk after dinner every evening; it is the one time that belongs to them alone. They usually take a few minutes at the outset of their walk, before they get distracted by other things, to kythe with each other. While they are connected in spiritual union they take turns mentioning some of their concerns: a sick friend, a couple whose marriage is in trouble, their children's schoolwork and health, their own commitments to each other, their professional work, and so on. They close their moment of communion with a gentle kiss.

Married couples can learn to kythe whenever they kiss. In this way, your kiss becomes a symbol of your spiritual union. People have told us that when they kiss this way, it becomes a very conscious and spiritual act of loving. Their kisses become an affirmation of their loving relationship rather than a perfunctory and mindless act.

Kything is especially powerful while dancing. The Sufi have developed a form of heart-to-heart dancing designed for two people who are deeply in love. During the dance, stand close to each other, face to face. Place your right hand, palm flat and facing outward, over your partner's heart (in the middle of the chest). And when your partner has placed his or her right hand over your heart, cover that hand with your own left hand. Remaining in this position and gazing into your partner's open eyes, move your feet in very small steps in time with the slow music, so that as a unit you turn ever so slowly in a continuous clockwise circle. When dancing this way, it may seem as though the other dancers on the dance floor have disappeared, and that you and your partner are joined at the eyes and at the heart into one soul.

In the sacrament of marriage two persons join together in loving union. The Bible describes the moment as the two "becoming one flesh," so deep is the union viewed by the Church. Married couples are uniquely suited to practice a coinherence kythe, where the two persons become "one flesh" without losing their identities. (See p.125 for a discussion of the coinherence kythe.)

A Tool for Spiritual Growth

Today, people seriously intent on spiritual growth are adopting spiritual tools which were formerly used only by professional religious people, such as meditation, contemplation, spiritual journal-keeping, and retreats. They are also adopting, adapting, and developing other practices as well. Some of these, including liturgical dance, laying on of hands, dreamwork, speaking in tongues, and chanting, are spiritual traditions rediscovered from earlier Judeo-Christian eras. Others, adapted from Eastern religious traditions for Christian use, include a wide range of yoga and zen exercises. Still others, based on current knowledge of psychological and spiritual dynamics, might be described as new discoveries. Among these are the spiritual practices of visualization, centering, affirmations and artwork, as well as the use of audio-visuals and music to facilitate contemplation.

In any field of endeavor—business, art, music, literature, statesmanship, science, physical fitness, mental health, etc.—having good intentions is not enough to bring about expertise and mastery. You must develop your skills and techniques through practice. It is no different in the spiritual life.

Technicians of the Sacred

Creating and improving spiritual practices to help people relate to each other and to God is the task of the spiritual scientist, or technician of the sacred. Ignatius Loyola, founder of the Jesuits, was a sixteenth century technician of the spiritual life. In the very first paragraph of his book *The Spiritual Exercises* he wrote, "Just as strolling, walking, and running are bodily exercises, so spiritual exercises are methods of preparing and disposing the soul." The rest of his book is filled with a regimen of suggested activities designed to produce spiritual growth in those who practice them.

While spirituality writers and theologians primarily generate ideas, concepts, theories, and theologies to help understand the spiritual life, technicians of the sacred, like Ignatius, assume the task of developing spiritual tools, techniques, methods, exercises, and practices designed to foster growth in the spiritual life. Kything is one of these spiritual tools, and we hope you will use its technology to enhance your spiritual growth.

Kything is an act of your soul or spirit. Others might say it is an act of your heart, your inner self, your core, or the center of your being. Each of these terms is an attempt to describe something that operates beyond your psychological faculties. To kythe means to let your heart or spirit manifest itself directly to another without any mask or disguise. Precisely speaking, kything refers to a direct spirit-to-spirit presence rather than to an indirect communication where I tell you how my heart feels and you tell me how your heart feels. Kything happens not principally in the psychological world but in the spiritual world.

At the level of spirit and soul we are all equals. Whenever you kythe with another person it is from a position of equality and reciprocity. In kything, you are always a receiver as well as a giver, a learner as well as a teacher, loved as well as loving. As a basic spiritual technique kything gives you access to communion and, through communion, to the spiritual world.

Developing Communion Skills

You can build your communion skills just as you can develop your communication skills, through training and practice. For example, at present, most of the people who kythe are unskilled in detecting the spiritual presence of another, unless they are physically present to the other, in dialogue with them, or holding a very strong image of the union. Thus, if I were to kythe with you right now without telling you, you probably could not consciously detect my loving presence. Here, then, is a very obvious area where we all need to develop our sensitivity and skill. We need to build a conscious line of communication between our spirit and our conscious ego-awareness, so that we can sense and know when another's spirit is present to us. A very basic spiritual skill is the skill of knowing when you are "in tune" with another soul.

A new trumpet player may develop the skill of producing notes on his instrument, but as soon as he wishes to make music with other musicians, he must set his instrument in tune with all their instruments. Even beginners can tell when their instrument is grossly out of tune, but only a trained musician can tune his instrument so that it is perfectly in tune with all the others.

At first, the bandleader must provide the trained ear for the trumpet player, telling the young musician whether or not his instrument is playing out of tune with the band. If the trumpet note is sharp or flat the leader tells the trumpet player to pull out the tuning slide a bit or push it in, and then to sound the tuning note again to see if it is in tune with the others. This procedure may need to be repeated three or four times before the instrument is in perfect alignment with the others.

Eventually, the trumpet player himself learns to hear when he is out of tune and when he is in tune, and he is able to adjust his own instrument to make his sound be in perfect union with the others.

Just as trumpet players learn to recognize when they are in tune, so persons who kythe learn to recognize when they are spiritually present to another, when they are "in tune." The goal would be to recognize when someone not in your physical presence was initiating a kythe with you, so that not only would your spirit be welcoming that person but your conscious mind would also be in touch with the new presence, and affirm it.

Ideally, the young musician also learns to recognize whether or not anyone else in the band is out of tune. Then, like the bandleader, he can help others get in tune and confidently affirm that they are in tune with each other. In a similar way you can hope eventually to become so sensitive to spiritual presence that you could recognize it even when it is happening around you—or anywhere, in fact. In a way, you would be developing your spiritual eyes and ears.

As you begin to practice kything you will begin to grow more sensitive in discerning the spiritual presence of others. During a practice session in a kything workshop Marie attempted to kythe with a male colleague of hers, a longtime professional associate and friend who had been married just the day before. In her attempt to kythe with him Marie discovered that her connection imagery spontaneously changed so that she saw him spiritually joined to his new wife. They came to Marie *together.* When Marie found herself in this unexpected spiritual presence, by shifting her imagery she reasserted that she had intended to kythe only with him, but her intention seemed to have little effect on the couple's communion because the image of the couple returned to her imagination. It was clear that the couple were joined and that if Marie wanted to kythe with him, she would have to kythe with both of them, which she did.

In this experience you can see that Marie is already developing her spiritual eyes and is able to recognize nuances of presence in the spiritual world.

The following chapter presents a number of questions people typically ask about kything. You may read our answers to these questions. Then, in the following four major sections of the book, you will explore how kything can affect your physical life, your psychological life, your spiritual life, and that domain of life we call the sacred.

5. Questions and Answers About Kything

Here are some of the most frequently asked questions about kything.

How old does a person have to be to do kything? Can children kythe?

Children naturally kythe and want to kythe. As long as children are mature enough to be able to sense their soul or spirit and desire to be connected in love to another person, they can be taught to kythe—how to initiate a kythe and how to welcome another's kythe. Once they learn the three basic steps described in Chapter 2—*Center, Focus, and Connect*—they can kythe as well as anyone.

Who can kythe? Who are capable of kything?

Anyone who has a loving heart and acknowledges the reality of the spiritual world can learn to kythe effectively. Kything is a natural ability, like communicating. It is also a natural right. One does not have to belong to a religious community to be able to kythe, nor does it require professional training. Kything as a loving spiritual way of connecting is a natural and developable skill and usually improves with practice.

How does kything feel?

The words most often used to describe the kything state of consciousness include: love, peace, freedom, union, stillness, harmony, connectedness, energy, indwelling, merging, closeness. People deeply in kythe generally lose their sense of time. They also often feel connected to all things. In this state they also want the best for the other person. They feel no sense of evil in the experience; it is as if evil has no meaning or possible existence in this state. Kything feels like—and is—primarily a new state of being. In a word, you feel that your soul is present to another's soul in a loving way.

Could kything be something I already know and do? Is kything a new way to be spiritually present to someone?

You can probably recall experiences in your own life that fit the definition of kything. Many of our students say they have been kything for years but never knew a word for it or never did it in precisely the way we describe here. In class they express delight, and sometimes relief, at finally having a name for their experiences of spiritual presence. Many others have wished they could experience, or imagined being able to experience kything. What this book does is explain how to kythe systematically and effectively, and show how broadly applicable kything can be.

We're not sure kything deserves the name "new." Since kything is a natural, normal act of the human spirit which anyone can do and which does not require any kind of extraordinary ability, it is often a spontaneous and frequent happening and feels quite familiar to many people.

Are there other ways to be spiritually present to someone?

Kything is merely one of a number of ways to be spiritually present to someone. Some other formal ways include sacramental communion, mystical rapture, membership in the communion of saints, and certain forms of spiritual healing. Spiritual presence also often occurs informally. For example, there are moments when intimate friends feel so close that they could say as Augustine did, "We are like two souls in a single body." Likewise, most people will remember stories of a parent (or child) having a sense that something important has happened to an absent family member. Twins too are frequently outstandingly able to experience each other's pain or joy at the moment it occurs, even when the pair are physically apart. And most of us have said to someone dear to us, "My heart goes with you."

Or we have asked them, "Please hold me in your heart." These are all examples of ways that people commonly refer to spiritual presence.

Whenever our friend Robin would say something hurtful to someone, she would ask, "Did I hurt your heart?" Evidently she understood that she could touch another's spirit with her words.

What are the best times and places for kything?

You can kythe at any time, no matter where you are. You may kythe when you are ill or healthy, happy or sad, fearful or confident, angry or joyful. Since kything is a spiritual event, you can kythe despite your emotional or mental state. Physically, you may be busy or bored, exhausted or full of energy, alone or in a large group, with a friend or an enemy; none of these physical conditions really prohibits you from kything, if you want to be spiritually connected to someone.

The best times to kythe are when you can afford to take some minutes to get centered and to enjoy the process to the fullest. We suggest using meditation time or at least part of it to practice kything formally, i.e., going through the three steps consciously. Also, when you are in church or take part in public services you usually have plenty of time to practice kything. (See Part V: Kything and the Sacred.)

Can I kythe with someone who is not physically present?

Yes. In fact, this is the most usual form of kything. When people you care about are not physically present and you miss them or are concerned and worried about them, you want to feel connected to them. If possible, you would like to support them, affirm them, and give them the strength and confidence they may need to do what they want to do. Kything is a very natural technique for accomplishing this. One woman kythed with her sister during the delivery of her baby, wishing her safety and health. One father kythed with the fetus of his unborn child while it was in the mother's womb. Another woman kythed with her daughter who was driving during a severe snowstorm. Another kythed with a friend who needed confidence in getting through a job interview. Another kythed with his son while he took a major exam, and with his daughter who was afraid she would get lost driving to a new destination. Another woman who missed her husband away on a business trip kythed with him each evening.

How long does it take to establish a kythe? How long should I stay in kythe with someone?

For beginners, we suggest you allow yourself at least ten minutes to go through the three steps of the kything process: *Center, Focus, and Connect.* After you have practiced the process formally a number of times, you can gauge your own timing. If you consistently kythe with the same persons, you will probably learn to establish a spiritual connection in a matter of moments. Once you have created a state of communion, you may remain in it as long as you wish.

Time, however, is not the most important factor in the state of communion. While some people cannot consciously sustain the kything state for more than a few moments, others create imagery to enrich the kything state and seem able to maintain and feel the connection for minutes, or even longer. But do not be misled by the intensity of the imagery or the "feel." The act of union is effected by *choice*. By choice you enter a kythe and by choice you leave it. In this sense, then, you can enter a kythe and choose to remain spiritually bonded much longer than your imagery or your attention can sustain it. We cannot emphasize enough that time is not the relevant factor. The goodness or effectiveness of a kythe is not measured by the length of time you can stay conscious of the communion, but by your ability to establish the union and choose it.

Is it possible for two people to remain in permanent kythe?

Precisely speaking, no. A kythe is by definition a conscious act of presence. It is initiated by a conscious choice and usually terminated by a conscious choice. *A spiritual bond or connection implies a permanence that is far longer than the few moments of spiritual presence usually associated with kything.* It is certainly possible to establish a permanent spiritual bond with someone, and use kything to initiate the connection. For example, if you had a son or daughter, as Patricia did, who was to be traveling alone in East Asia for three months, you might want to establish a permanent spiritual bond with your child, and in addition from time to time you might want to use kything consciously to spiritually reconnect for a few minutes with him or her.

In this light, when couples take their marriage vows, whether they realize it or not, they are choosing to establish a permanent spiritual bond with each other. Kything is valuable in helping bring this permanent bond into awareness and to renew it. Certain Christian couples have also made Christ a third member, so to speak, of their marriage union, so that both individually and as a couple they are joined in permanent communion with Christ and, in Christ, with each other.

Faithful Christians are always in permanent spiritual connection to Christ. And certain mystics have described their relationship with Christ as an eternal spiritual marriage. In this sense, whenever I consciously choose to kythe with Christ, it adds an extra dimension of awareness and presence to the permanent spiritual bond I already enjoy with Christ.

Can I kythe with more than one person at a time? Can a group of people kythe together?

Yes, to both questions. There seems to be no limit to the number of spiritual connections you can make and sustain. There are no special skills needed to kythe with more than one person. At first, we recommend you use *additive kything,* that is, kythe first with one person, then add another and another, and so on, until you hold all the persons together in your imagery. Far from diminishing the sense of bondedness, additive kything can intensify the experience. When kything is used for healing, the intensity produced by a group of people kything with a sick person can be very powerful.

What is the best way to start kything, to build confidence in my ability to kythe?

Begin kything with a partner you love and trust, and do it when you are both physically present to each other. Take enough time so that both of you can experience being initiator and receiver of the kythe.

At first, tell each other when you are at each step of the process, so

47

that you can be sensitive to the other's experience. When people are physically present to you, it is often easier to feel their spiritual presence, especially if both of you are centered. If they are consciously waiting for you to kythe with them, they are likely to feel the moment when your spirit becomes focused on them. With practice you can learn to distinguish spiritual presence from physical presence and even from physical touch. There is an American Indian courtship ritual in which the man and woman sit silently next to each other for hours, never touching and never looking at each other. To people who do not understand the ritual, their behavior may seem odd or meaningless, but to the couple it is their chance to learn to be spiritually present to each other, to get to know each other's souls without any confusing factors of physical touching or psychological communicating.

Does kything always happen?

Once in a rare while your attempt to kythe may not succeed. This phenomenon is most noticeable when you initiate a kythe and the other person does not welcome your spirit. The event seems to occur in the following manner: You initiate a kythe in which you are directing the focus of your spiritual presence toward the other person. Metaphorically speaking, your spirit seems to go out toward the other but instead of coming to rest there, your spirit seems to bounce back to you as if it had hit a rubber wall.

Jesus described this phenomenon in a similar way. When he was giving instructions to his disciples going off to their missions, he told them, "Whatever house you go into, let your first words be, 'Peace to this house!' If a person of peace lives there, *your peace will go and rest on that person; if not, it will come back to you"* (Luke 10:5–6). It seems clear Jesus was talking about initiating a spiritual connection, and was acknowledging that at times such an offer might be rejected.

Most of us are not consciously spiritually sensitive enough to sense when a loving spirit is present to us and when it is not. Nevertheless, your soul or spirit is indeed sensitive to that presence. Your spirit will not welcome a soul by which it feels threatened, even though you may not be conscious of your spirit rejecting the other—or being rejected by another.

What should I do when I can't seem to make a kythe connection?

If you are initiating a kythe by focusing your spiritual presence on the other person and you seem to get rebuffed for no apparent reason, try another approach. Imagine yourself as the locus of the kythe. Perhaps in the first case the other person's spirit felt afraid of being invaded, so to speak, and closed itself off to you. In the alternate approach, the other person may allow his or her spiritual presence to come to you. This situation is like the person who doesn't invite you into his home, but is willing to come into yours.

One alternative is to kythe with a third person who would act as a link or mediator between you and the resistant kyther. A woman tried kything with one of her relatives who generally mistrusted her. She was unable to effect a kythe with him in the usual way. However, she was quite ingenious. She knew the man was very devoted to Francis of Assisi, so she kythed with the saint first, and together they were able to establish a kythe with the relative. If this doesn't work either, we suggest you imagine the kything happening in a neutral "place" such as a meadow, a sacred building or out in space. At another time, this persistent woman kythed with the same relative by imaging them together at an ocean beach they had both known. She was also successful kything with him when she envisioned them together at a pine woods in Vermont that she felt he would like.

How do I expand my kything skills?

Practice kything with a number of different people in order to develop your spiritual sensitivities. Notice how differently it feels to kythe with children, with the very old, with the sick, with the handicapped, with the lonely, with the very busy, with people you know intimately, and with people who are strangers. Kything offers you a way of lovingly reaching out and touching the lives of others. It adds a spiritual component to your life and a spiritual connection to the world.

Are people aware of it when you kythe with them?

People do not have to know beforehand that you are going to kythe with them. If they know you and love you, their spirit is usually open to your loving presence, even if their conscious mind is busy with other matters. At the level of everyday consciousness, most people are not sensitive enough to be aware that you are spiritually present to them. Usually, only those who are centered or those who are expecting your spirit's presence ever feel anything.

However, you may eventually develop your spiritual sensitivity so that you can become just as aware of someone's spiritual presence as you are of his or her physical presence. Jesus, for example, was aware when he was touched at the level of spirit even though he was physically and mentally otherwise involved. "Somebody touched me," Jesus said. "I felt power go out from me" (Luke 8:46).

Can I communicate—be telepathic—when I kythe with another person?

Many people have reported spontaneous experiences of telepathy while kything. In Madeleine L'Engle's novel *A Wind in the Door,* the angelic cherubim Proginoskes treated telepathy as very elementary in kything. Structurally, if you are spiritually connected with someone, it would seem very logical that you could influence each other's physical and mental lives. At times the spiritual connection seems to overflow into the psychological or physical domains, for example, when after kything I feel a new confidence or have a clear sense of what to say or how to act in a difficult situation, or I feel stronger physically or begin physically to heal. In this "overflow" sense, telepathy would seem to be a possible outcome of a kything relationship. We have not researched this phenomenon because our interest is primarily in developing the ability to be spiritually present to another person, which is the essence of kything.

Can a person's body or mind be healed through kything?

Apparently, yes. Most forms of spiritual healing presume spiritual presence, i.e., some form of kything or communion. What healers disagree about is exactly how spiritual healing takes place, and why. Some feel that spiritual energy is transmitted from healer to healee. Other healers claim they are only a channel for some more powerful healing force in the universe, e.g., God or nature. Still other healers claim they do not transfer or direct the flow of energy at all; they just establish a simple spirit-to-spirit presence, and this presence releases the innate self-healing abilities of the healee. Healers seem to agree that as a primary step in healing they experience an unconditional love toward the healee. The relation between kything and healing is discussed more fully in Part II: Kything and the Physical.

Can I kythe with plants and animals?

You can kythe with anything that possesses a soul or spiritual dimension. Traditional philosophy has always taught that, while humans alone possess *rational souls,* animals possess *animal souls,* and plants, flowers, and trees possess *vegetative souls.* (Those soul names were first given by Aristotle.) Since humans lack an adequate way to communicate with plants and animals, it would seem that spiritual presence provides a very natural and valid way for people to relate to these creatures. We have found some loving and inspiring stories told about kything with animals, trees, and flowers. See Part IV: Kything and the Spiritual for some stories and suggestions for kything with nature.

Can kything be used with evil intentions?

By definition, to be in kythe is to be in an open and loving relationship. Since the kything state is defined as a state of consciousness characterized by openness and unconditional love, you cannot kythe with evil intentions. To claim such an ability is a contradiction in terms. You cannot choose to be in a state of unconditional love and simultaneously choose to have evil intentions. There is no need to fear that destructive spiritual energy can be present in a kything communion. The desire to build loving union and the desire to destroy it cannot be part of the same act. The destructive intention cannot exist as long as the loving one is present. Other people may use occult spiritual practices such as voodoo and evil eye with malevolent intentions. Whatever state of consciousness these practices require, it is not the state of unconditional love where kything happens. Kything is not an occult practice. It is a skill for bringing loving relationships into being.

Spiritual power, however, covers a much broader area than kything. Like any power, spiritual energy can be misused and abused or even used destructively. Technically, praying for someone and putting a curse on someone are actions which both take place in the spiritual world. Spiritual energy exists and it is neutral. Just as we learned to use physical energies such as electricity and magnetism wisely, and to use psychological energies such as logic and intuition wisely, we need to learn to use spiritual energies wisely. Kything is designed to bring awareness of spiritual energy into consciousness and to use it constructively, both for personal growth and for the growth of the human community. Since, with kything, we are taking an evolutionary step by making communion conscious, we can look forward to an era of highly complex consciousness and an exquisite interpersonal potential throughout the human species.

When you kythe do you lose a sense of your own identity? In becoming one with another do you lose your self?

If anything, in kything you learn to be consciously in touch with the spiritual dimensions of your whole self and are empowered in the process. In kything you come to have a fuller sense of who you are and how you are connected to others and to all reality. Teilhard de Chardin, one of this century's most influential theologians, pointed out that in the domain of spirit "union differentiates." That is, the "law of oneness" states that the closer two people truly grow in spiritual union, the clearer their own individualities are recognized and differentiated. In other words the more deeply you enter into union with another, the more fully you become yourself. Far from suppressing your uniqueness and individuality, the union produced by kything enhances it.

What does happen in kything is that you develop a new orientation to reality. You begin to see the vastness of the world of relationships. From a Christian perspective, once you understand and practice kything you can, perhaps for the first time, understand what the communion of saints is all about, realize that you are an essential member of that immense spiritual network, and take an active role in carrying out its grand purpose, which is to achieve loving unity among all that exists.

Kything and the Physical

6. Kything and the Body

The Mistaken Limits of Physical Presence

Culturally we are taught to believe that our physical presence ends at our skin, but it has much wider boundaries than that, even by strict physical definition. We define something as physically present to us if we can taste, touch, see, smell or hear it. Consider each sense-presence in turn to gain a true sense of our physical boundaries.

Recall how far physical presence extends when it is recognized by the sense of *smell*. Even when you close your eyes, you know when you are physically present to a bouquet of carnations across the room. The physical presence of the flowers by means of their aroma reaches far beyond the boundaries of their stems and petals. In a similar way when you are out driving you are physically present to skunks by their odor even though the smelly creatures may be half a mile away. So a skunk's physical presence is at least a mile in diameter.

Consider how the sense of *hearing* also helps truly define your physical boundaries. For example, you are physically present to your friend who hears you shouting to him from his front yard, far beyond the boundaries of your skin. When he heard your car horn tooting in front of his house a few moments before, he knew that somebody was physically present. But as soon as he heard your voice shouting, he acknowledged *your* physical presence.

With the telephone, physical presence through the sense of hearing becomes almost limitless. A telephone provides a quality of personal presence far different from the experience of listening to a tape recorded mes-

55

sage on a telephone-answering device. When I converse with you on the phone, I can verify your physical presence at that moment even though you may be thousands of miles away.

The sense of *sight* offers another example of the long reach of physical presence. Standing on your front porch you can be visibly present to your friend as he walks down the street toward your house. *Your physical presence extends as far as you are visible.* In a similar way, the moon is physically present to you as are the stars. They evoke a physical response from your eyes.

But your true physical size appears only to be hinted at when you use the physical senses. Realizing that your physical presence stretches out to the front yard or even many miles away is only a token of your physical reality, according to modern physicists. Recent advances in radioisotope techniques make it possible to trace the chemical elements that enter and leave the human body, either through the skin, by elimination or by breathing.

It seems that over 95% of the ten octillion atoms in your body are replaced annually. Some body parts such as bone tissue are eroded and reformed quickly, while the brain's connective cells are more resistant to being replaced. But, without a doubt, after five years you are totally repackaged chemically, renewed down to the very last atom. So, explained Brad Lemley in an article called "Biodance," "If you are thirty years old and looking at a photo of yourself as a newborn baby, that was six bodies ago."[1]

According to Dr. Larry Dossey, a diagnostician and researcher, breathing plays an important part in this dance of life. One estimate he reports suggests that due to the thorough mixing of the earth's atmosphere, every time you inhale you are taking in at least one atom of air breathed by each and every person on earth within the last few weeks. "That air is carried by the lungs into the bloodstream. It becomes a part of you," says Dossey. So your breathing contains nothing less than "a low-frequency chain of chemical contact between all living humans past and present."[2] You might even allow yourself to think that your body has no beginning and no ending.

---

[1] Brad Lernley, "Biodance," *The Washington Post Magazine,* Feb. 23, 1986, p. 10.
[2] *Ibid.*

When the physicists talk like that to us we begin to wonder what is "myself"? Perhaps your consciously-shared spiritual presence in kything is already experienced, certainly unconsciously, as a physical oneness in this dance of life.

When you speak of the boundaries of physical presence, then, it is important not to limit the magnificent radius of your physical presence—or that of anyone or anything else.

Normally, of course, you refer to others as being physically present when they are near enough so that you could reach out and *touch* them with your hands. Physical touching of someone you love can be a very powerful experience, one that you miss when it is not available. This awareness suggests a simple way to use kything.

Kything To Bring Comfort

Suppose you come home from work with a stiff neck and you are alone. You are apt to rub or massage your stiff neck. Given your wish you probably would prefer to have someone else doing the massage. Wouldn't it be nice if someone you loved was helping you work out your stress and tension?

What you can do is kythe with that loving person in such a way that, as you worked your fingers around the soreness in your neck, it would also feel like the fingers of the loving person massaging you in and through his or her spirit. Using your imagination to facilitate the process, picture the other person massaging your neck. As you continue to rub, imagine the other person comforting you, wanting you to relax, and helping you let go of the stiffness. In this way, massaging your stiff neck becomes transformed into an act of spiritual presence.

In times of high anxiety and pressure people sometimes spontaneously hug themselves, perhaps as a remembrance of being hugged protectively in childhood. In such stressful times you may kythe with someone you would like to have hugging you, as you hug yourself.

Similarly, if you know that someone is alone and in need of comforting, you may kythe with him or her. A woman kythed herself to her absent daughter by picturing herself combing her daughter's hair. Combing her daughter's hair had always been a time of quiet closeness between the two of them. Kything provided an opportunity for the mother to make those remembered moments of closeness come alive again for her in communion with her daughter. The imaginative picture of combing her daughter's hair merely facilitated the kythe and helped focus her spiritual presence.

People usually associate spiritual presence with very specific memories, objects, places, and certain activities, as this mother did with combing her daughter's hair and as the young boy in Chapter 1 did with wearing his grandfather's cap and sitting in his favorite chair.

Kything Using Physical Touch

In our workshops on kything, we often invite participants to kythe with each other using physical touch as a way to get them focused on the kything process. If you were in our workshop, we would ask you to sit behind someone and, after you had gotten centered, to rest your hands on the shoulders of your partner. Next, we would ask you to project the focus of your spirit into your own hands, and to take a moment to experience what it felt like to be centered in your hands. Learning to place the focus of your spiritual presence in your hands is a useful skill, as it provides a starting point for many kinds of kything, for example, massaging someone's stiff neck, combing someone's hair, and working with healing energy.

Once you had focused the presence of your spirit into your hands, we would then ask you, in a context of unconditional loving, to change this focus from your hands *to your partner.* We would ask you to imagine your spiritual presence (without saying anything) moving through your partner's skin, so to speak, and into his or her body and heart. This is what we call a *touching kythe.* If your partner is also quiet and centered, he or she can usually identify the moment when your shift of focus takes place, when you project your spiritual presence, so to speak, *into* him or her.

During one of our workshops a woman participant was in the midst of a grieving process for a friend who had recently died. "When Barbara and I were doing the touching kythe," she explained, "there was a feeling of warmth, love, compassion, and of being connected to a power beyond ourselves. I felt very peaceful for the first time since the death of my friend two weeks ago."

Once the state of communion is established, you may remove your hands from your partner's back or shoulders, or keep them there. Whatever physical movement you then make, or do not make, will usually have little effect on the state of communion established by kything. This shift of spiritual focus is carried out by your intention or conscious choice. Thus, whether or not you have removed your hands from your partner's back, you may choose to continue kything or to stop.

When you choose to stop kything and to remove your spirit from its communion with your partner's spirit, your partner will probably feel the shift and sense the withdrawal of your spiritual presence.

Because this withdrawal is usually clearly felt by the partner, it is often a turning point for people who are not sure if they "believe in" kything or the reality of spiritual presence. The receptive partner is usually the one who most clearly feels the difference between being in and out of communion with another.

We usually ask the same partners to practice starting and stopping the kythe a number of times, till they grow accustomed to feeling the partner's spiritual presence or lack of it.

Then we ask partners to change roles—the up-front partner now takes a sitting position behind the other—and repeat the entire procedure. Afterward we ask them to discuss the experience.

Some report finding the kything experience new and revolutionary. Others who have been kything naturally all their lives talk about it as a familiar experience. During the kything communion many report physical sensations such as warmth, coolness, tingling or vibrations. Some other characteristic responses include feeling calm, peaceful, comforted, loved, and cherished. When a partner's spiritual presence is withdrawn, people most often describe it as a feeling of "emptiness" or "loss."

Many of those who had been hesitant or even scared to try kything found it a loving, peaceful experience—even awesome. Through kything, some participants even reached a level of spiritual intimacy—communion without communication—they had never experienced before and of which they never thought themselves capable. "I was never fully present to someone's soul before this experience," one participant said, "and I was filled with reverence and awe."

After this experience, many workshop participants began practicing kything in their daily lives.

Kything and Physical Exercise

A good time to practice kything is when you are doing physical exercise, especially when the task does not demand your rational attention, for example, when swimming, jogging, jumping, pedaling a stationary bicycle or walking alone.

People have reported a variety of ways they kythe during physical exercise. "I have a group of people with whom I kythe each day," explained a young executive. "I kythe with them one at a time as I exercise."

Another said, "I kythe with my fitness instructor and in spirit ask her to teach me the best way to exercise. I want her to share with me her spirit of determination so that I will persevere in my program. When I work out at home I picture her next to me doing all the exercises I do and coaching me."

Another kythes with his yoga instructor, asking him to supervise the practice session and to share with him his patience and spiritual motivation.

Another kythes with an absent friend. "I really miss her," she explained, "and I know she'd love to be with me, so I picture her jogging beside me and I enjoy her spiritual presence. I've also been enjoying jogging more since I began to do it in kythe with my friend."

An executive who has access to a pool during lunch hour says he kythes with his wife while he swims. "She loves being in the water even more than I do," he explained, "so I take her with me in spirit whenever I jump into the pool. Kything with her allows me to express my feelings of love for her, my delight in her, and my wish that she were here enjoying the pool with me. Kything has helped me to love her and value her in new ways."

Another who takes dancing class for physical exercise says she kythes with world-famous dancers and imagines them sharing their rhythm with her as she dances. "It frees my spirit," she said, "and I feel really connected to those super dancers. It's as if I know them in a special way and have become friends with them. And I am sure, if I ever had a chance to ask them to encourage and support me, they would do it."

Kything for Novel Physical Experiences

What if you can't dance or do gymnastics or don't have a pool to swim in? Can you still participate in spirit in such activities? The answer is "yes."

Kythe with someone who may be a graceful dancer on a ballroom floor, or an Olympic gymnast executing a breathtaking routine, or a swimmer enjoying the ocean's waves. Through kything let your spirit help you discover what it feels like to be dancing, exercising, swimming, or whatever it is you would like to experience physically.

A woman we know who is paralyzed reported that she frequently kythes with the gymnasts and other athletes while watching sporting events on television. "Instead of feeling left out," she said, "kything lets me feel like a part of those wonderful young bodies as they move gracefully and effortlessly before my eyes."

A husband wanted to know what it felt like physically and emotionally to be his pregnant wife, so he kythed with her. "It was so different from just looking at her from the outside as I had always done before," he explained. "When I kythed I really felt I was inside her. For instance, I became aware from within how the weight of the baby made her stand and walk the way she did to keep her balance. I understood her a lot more when she told me how the baby felt. I loved her and our baby in a new way. I felt closer to them than I ever had."

A young man who jogged every morning before work often thought about his favorite uncle, who was recovering from a stroke but his left side was still not responding. In a spirit of love for his uncle, the young man would kythe with him as he jogged and picture the half-paralyzed man running in his young body. "It was both Uncle Chet and I running together in my body," the young man explained. "Funny, sometimes I could even sense my left side, his paralyzed side, holding me back. As 'we' ran, I would encourage him inside me by saying, 'Come on, man, you can do it.' "

No matter what kind of human activity you may wish to experience, you may use kything to help you. It takes only a few moments to grow quiet and centered, then to use your imagination to facilitate the spiritual connection you desire. Once connected in a loving communion, the agenda is up to you—or to the spirits of both you and your kything partner.

Sick People and Physical Presence

Sick people, especially when their illness is serious or uncertain, usually feel frightened and alone. Often enough their physical recovery is coming along fine. What's missing is the felt presence of someone who loves and cares. This presence need not always be physical.

Ill people sometimes have mixed feelings about being in the physical presence of others, especially certain others. Some who are sick in bed with an ordinary illness such as a cold or the flu don't want other people around; they prefer to be left alone. Nevertheless they do like to know that there is someone who cares. On the other hand, some people ill at home really appreciate physical presence and are especially conscious of their loneliness, pain or anxiety when no one is around.

For both kinds of sick people kything offers a satisfying experience. The kind who prefer to remain physically alone may kythe with others as much or as often as they desire. Or they may welcome family and friends to initiate a kythe with them. "Keep me in mind and say a prayer for me," is the way one person expressed it. Another said, "I find it very reassuring to know there is someone who wants to stay in kythe with me."

The kind who prefer having others physically present give friends like you an opportunity. Even though you may not be able to be with them physically, say, in the hospital this afternoon, you can agree to kythe with them. Presence is important even if it can only be spiritual presence. It offers to sick and alone persons a sense of groundedness in a loving relationship.

It helps if both of you agree upon a certain time to kythe, so that the act of communion is planned as a very specific event and consciously carried out. In this way kything keeps you aware of each other, of your connectedness to each other, as well as of your compassion and care for each other.

Of course, when you arrive at the hospital and are physically present in the room, you may also kythe with the sick person then, to deepen your sense of presence to each other.

Kything Without Interfering in Another's Life

The primary purpose of kything is spiritual presence: a compassionate, caring, unconditionally loving presence. When you kythe with someone, you want the highest and the best for him or her. At the same time, your unconditional love for such persons has no place in it for wanting to control, manipulate or interfere with their life.

Often when people are ill they are going through a psychological process of growth and responsibility. They face questions that may not occur to them when they are healthy and busy. At times they experience many unwelcome feelings of insecurity, confusion, and even anger at their illness. Compassionate kything allows their growth process to happen without trying to control it.

When people are terminally ill, they normally go through a five-stage process of dying, outlined by Dr. Elisabeth Kübler-Ross in her book *On Death and Dying.* Kything is not meant to interfere with that important process but to support the dying person through it, at whatever stage the person may happen to be. One of these stages involves expressing anger at the dying process. As you kythe with dying persons, even though you may feel uncomfortable sensing their anger, you can still envision health for them. You can also affirm their process of letting go of physical life as a way to step into a new life.

Traditionally, people near death have often wanted their friends and family physically present. Stories are told of monks and nuns whose communities gathered around their deathbeds. In such scenes spontaneous

63

kything often took place. Frequently the dying person reported an awareness (or even a vision) of Christ or saints of the heavenly court. Beside the physical presence of the earthly community standing in the room there was the spiritual presence of the heavenly community.

If you are standing near the bed of a dying person, you may kythe with the person. Kything would intensify your physical presence and enable you to join the dying person at a profound level.

If you cannot be physically present at the deathbed of a close relative or friend, you can kythe with that person. Gift him or her with courage and compassion from wherever you are. At the very least, you can establish communion with the person and experience each other's presence.

One of our workshop participants told us, "During the exercise, I kythed with a close friend overseas. In her last letter she told me she hasn't long to live, and I thank God I can be with her in this way. I plan to write to her soon and tell her about kything and how we can do it together."

7. Kything and Self-Healing

Fostering Your Own Healing Process

When and how might you use kything to foster your own healing?

Although this section of the book focuses primarily on the physical effects of kything, you may follow the kything procedure outlined below for illnesses which may be physical, psychological, spiritual or some combination of the three.

Since humans are inextricably body, mind, and spirit all woven into one, your spiritual activity naturally has an effect on your body and mind. Although kything is primarily a spiritual activity, it can affect physical and mental activity—yours as well as those with whom you kythe.

You may need healing at a *spiritual* level if you are unable to forgive, insist on harboring a grudge, are overwhelmed by cowardice, are unable to be creative, compassionate, find meaning in your life or discern what is truly in your highest interests.

You may need healing at a *psychological* level if you are being disempowered by fear, anxiety, guilt, nervousness or confusion, if you are unable to think straight, if you frequently respond to situations with inappropriate anger, fear, distrust or other strong emotions, or if you are unable to be in touch with your feelings.

You may need healing at the *physical* level if you are in physical pain after an operation, dental work, or a severe burn, if you have frequent headaches, asthma, arthritis, and allergy bouts, if you suffer from chronic illness such as diabetes, high blood pressure, or heart condition, or if you are home from work for a day with a sore throat, a cold or the flu. Whether your

65

condition is simple or serious, you may enlist the help of your own self-healing powers in any of these contexts.

Kything, of course, is never meant to be a substitute for proper medical care of physical illness; what kything does call upon, in addition to the professional treatment of a physician, is your own choice to live as healthily as you can and the presence of a spiritual network that will support your commitment to that choice.

Steps for a Self-Healing Kythe

Ellie was a cook in a Mexican restaurant. One busy night she spilled some burning grease on her arm. Since the kitchen was bustling and she was in the midst of preparing four rush orders, she couldn't just drop everything and take care of her burn. So, she took a deep breath, closed her eyes for a second, and kythed with her mother who had taught her to kythe and who, she knew, could "take the pain out of burns." "I had to stay with my cooking until there was a lull in the rush," she explained. "When I closed my eyes, I pictured my mother with her hands over my burn saying 'I want your arm to be healthy.' It worked!" Ellie proudly related. "The kything took the pain away and I got the burn taken care of with the first aid kit fifteen minutes later."

Normally, a kythe for self-healing takes the following general steps:

1. **Choose a healing figure with whom you want to kythe.** It may be Christ, some holy person, a saint, a well-known healer or physician. Ellie chose her mother.

2. **Take enough time to grow quiet and centered.** This is a serious action and you will want to get as deeply into the kything experience as possible. Ellie had only a few seconds to get centered but it was enough. In moments of crisis like this it is often possible to establish a kythe in a few seconds.

3. **Express a simple choice to be healed, healthy, and whole.** Say aloud or to yourself, "I choose to be healthy and whole." This choice clearly

orients the kythe toward healing. Ellie made this choice when she called upon the spiritual presence of her mother who symbolized for her the healing choice, because she knew "she could take the pain out of burns."

4. **Kythe with the healing figure using the standard three steps: Get centered, focus on the other, and establish a connection.** Use your imagination to help you experience this union. Affirm the healing figure's presence and ability to help in the healing. Ellie used the image of her mother's healing hands touching her arm as a way of establishing connection.

5. **If you wish, you may focus your attention on the area needing to be healed.** To facilitate this, you may place your hand on or near the area to be healed and visualize the area fully healed and operating healthily.

6. **Remain in this consciously receptive mode for a few moments, or minutes, or as long as you wish.** Ellie had only a few moments before she had to get back to her cooking, but even while busy and with her eyes wide open she probably kept a lingering image of the kything union.

Note: If you lose your attention or get distracted during a kythe, gently refocus your attention and presence. There is no need to feel guilty or to reprimand yourself if you get distracted. It is quite normal. It happens to everyone.

Once a healing kythe is established, the spiritual bonding it produces continues to remain in effect even after you go back to your ordinary activities. Whenever you wish during the day, you may refocus, reaffirm, and refresh the healing kythe. You may also invite others into it. The healing process remains in effect until you choose to stop it.

Remember that in matters large and small your highest self, or soul, wants your health and knows best how to achieve and maintain it. So, allow your soul to go about the healing process in its own way. Your healing process will probably follow usual paths such as getting plenty of rest, taking medicine, and following the advice of a physician. It may also take some unexpected turns and unusual forms such as an unexplained remission of symptoms or the introduction of a new person into your life who brings compelling insights for your health.

Trust, too, that the persons with whom you choose to kythe also want your healing and wholeness, and that they have access to many healing resources unknown to you.

Ellie administered first aid to her burn as soon as she had a break. It is important to underline the fact that kything does not dispense with seeing physicians when necessary, nor does it substitute for taking normal care of your health. If, because of a heart condition, you are required to do moderate exercise for half an hour each day, no amount of kything will substitute for the required physical exercise.

In Ellie's case as in many others the purpose of kything is to establish a context of healing. Ellie did not want to avoid taking proper care of her burn. What kything did was allow her to be in communion with someone who could help her immediately. It also allowed her to realize, as part of the context of her healing, that there were others in the world who wanted her healing and happiness.

8. Helping Heal Others Through Kything

The Presence of a Healer

When a Tibetan physician does a pulse diagnosis on a patient, the physician creates a deep centering union between them that can only be based on a spiritual presence of empathic oneness. Such a moment was described by an American surgeon, Richard Selzer, watching a Tibetan doctor, Yeshi Donden, at work in an American hospital:

> For the next half hour he remains thus, suspended above the patient like some exotic golden bird with folded wings, holding the pulse of the woman beneath his fingers, cradling her hand in his. All the powers of the man seem to have been drawn down into this one purpose.... And I know that I, who have palpitated a hundred thousand pulses, have not truly felt a single one.[1]

Dr. Selzer then explained that the Tibetan physician went on to accurately diagnose a specific type of congenital heart disorder solely on the basis of taking the woman's pulse.

Although the Tibetan doctor did not *heal* the patient but merely diagnosed her, his diagnosis utilized not only his highly-developed skills but also a form of spiritual presence. The story points out that there are modes of healing presence that can complement today's scientific medical prac-

---

[1] Richard Selzer, "Yeshi Donden: The Tibetan Doctor," *Harper's,* January 1976.

tice. The American surgeon reverently acknowledged that the Tibetan had achieved a form of communion with that patient that he had never experienced.

Spiritual Healing

Throughout the centuries many varieties of spiritual healing have been used by different healers. Most of these procedures begin with the healer establishing a spiritual connection with the healee. Sometimes the healee is aware of the procedure, sometimes not. At times the healer is physically present to the healee; at other times only a spiritual connection is possible. The point is that once the healer has kythed with the healee the two of them are connected at the level of spirit. This communion provides a vehicle for spiritual healing.

To experts and theoreticians it is *not* clear how spiritual healing works. Some hypothesize that there is a *transfer* of energy from the healer to the healee. For example, when the woman with the flow of blood touched Jesus' cloak and was healed, Jesus recognized that energy had gone out of him.

Others who follow a second approach to spiritual healing see themselves merely as a *channel* for the healing, the energy for which comes from the universe or directly from God. Such healers describe healing energy as a power or force passing through them the way electricity might pass through an electrical power line. They see themselves as a conduit for energy that has its source in some remote power plant. The conduit paradigm seems to be most popular among faith healers and those who pray over the sick. Their prayer is *for God to do the healing.*

A third approach is to view a healing kythe simply as an act of communion *which releases self-healing capacities already present in the healee.* For those who follow this approach there is no transfer of energy from healer to healee to account for; there is no talk of "energy" at all nor of "sending energy" or "sending healing." Dr. Lawrence LeShan discussed this approach in his book, *The Medium, the Mystic, and the Physicist,* and called it Type I healing.[2]

When you think of healing and kything, what theoretical view should you hold? The transfer of energy? The channeling of energy? Or the release of the healee's self-healing capacities (Type I)?

Perhaps the best answer is to recommend that you experiment with each of the different approaches a number of times and discover which theoretical view best fits your personal experience. Whichever hypothesis or explanation turns out to be true—perhaps under different conditions all three perspectives are true—people have reported getting well from healers who follow each of them. Here are descriptions of ways to use a healing kythe with each approach.

1. Kything and Type I Healing

LeShan's Type I healing is perhaps the simplest, since it bypasses the questions that scientists ask spiritual healers: What is the nature of this healing energy? Where does it come from? How does it get from the healer to the healee when they are physically apart?

In this book, since we are presenting kything primarily as an act of spiritual presence and not as a tool for healing, we do not need to face those questions directly. However, since a scientist such as LeShan must design research and produce evidence to prove or disprove any hypothesis he proposes, these questions are important for those who choose to follow either the "transfer of energy" or the "channeling of energy" approaches. LeShan's Type I healing, which does not need to deal with the concept of energy, does not need to deal with these questions.

LeShan's Type I healing procedure follows almost exactly the three steps for initiating a kythe. He simply asks you to: (1) grow quiet and cen-

---

[2]Lawrence LeShan, *The Medium, the Mystic, and the Physicist: Toward a General Theory of the Paranormal.* New York: Ballantine Books, 1975, pp. 99ff.

tered, (2) focus your attention contemplatively and lovingly on the healee, and (3) become one with the healee.

He suggests using an imaginative symbol to picture this oneness. You might picture you and the healee holding hands or embracing, or being two branches from the same tree, two pieces of an interlocking puzzle, or whatever image of union which might be helpful to you at the moment.

In Type I healing the result that you as healer intend is that the two of you be in union in a context of love and peace. That is all. LeShan does not ask you to intend the healing of a particular wound or illness. If you follow this Type I approach, a LeShan healing action would be no more and no less than what we call a simple loving kythe.

LeShan believes that it takes a good deal of practice for people to learn how to do well each of the three steps: centering, contemplating a person, and establishing union. The hundreds of people who have been taught Type I healing by LeShan trainers over a long-weekend workshop have reported significant healing results.

Sometimes a certain amount of healing spontaneously takes place when two people are joined in a simple loving kythe. One of our workshop participants was Becky, a young woman graduate student paralyzed from the waist down. In class we assigned partners to practice kything with each other so that they could report to each other anything they felt during the process. Here's what Becky's partner reported:

The experience of kything with Becky as my partner was profound. I believe in the power of the spirit to heal, have known others involved in healings of this type, and have believed we all possess the power of the spirit within us to heal. But I had never been "involved." When kything with her I sensed or envisioned (words here are inadequate) that I was sitting in her wheelchair with her, my legs wrapped around her. My inner thighs felt power—energy! They felt as though they were shaking and vibrating. I felt very united to her. Afterward, when Becky told me that her kidney pain had left during this experience, I began to get a clearer understanding of what had happened and what kything can be.

As you learn to kythe, you will develop your own procedure and do it in your own way. One of our students described how she goes through the three basic steps of kything, and we liked it so much we thought we would share it here:

When I settle on the person with whom I want to kythe, I usually take two or three deep breaths to help me get relaxed and centered. Then, when I form an image of the person in my imagination, I breathe love and peace through my heart to that person. I imagine that the entire area of my heart is a breathing apparatus, but instead of inhaling and exhaling air, it breathes love and peace. As I breathe love to the person, I see him or her surrounded with a glowing circle of light. The circle of light I picture around the person isn't just of my making. It's mine, but it's more than mine. It represents universal love, or God's love, as well as my love. Finally, I picture the two of us together in that glowing light. When I can see us together in a circle of love, which is God's love, I usually say, "We are surrounded with light and love and the all-pervasive healing, guiding presence of God."

2. Kything as Channeling of Healing Energy

A second approach to spiritual healing talks about channeling energy. This is the most popular view. In it you see yourself not as the source of the healing energy but merely as the channel through which it flows. In his research LeShan reported that the largest group of healers described their work as "prayer" and believed their success was due to the intervention of God.[3] In this approach, you view yourself as a channel either of God's healing power or of a spiritual energy universally available. It is seen to be uni-

_____

[3]LeShan, *Ibid.,* p. 102.

73

versally available, in much the same way that solar energy, wind, magnetism, electricity, and other energies of a physical nature are universally available for those who know how to tap into them.

To do a healing kythe from within this framework begin as before by growing quiet and centered. Then, in the context of the divine presence or universal energy (often imaged as an atmosphere of light which may be colored white, silver, gold, transparent or some other hue), lovingly kythe with the healee.

Once the kythe is established you may affirm the oneness you share, express your unconditional love for the healee, and formulate a prayer for the healee's health. To do this you may introduce imagery into your kythe, such as seeing the divine light touch the person to be healed and picturing the area to be healed as cured, healthy, and functioning well.

If the person to be healed is physically present you may use your hands as a symbol of your channeling. Touch the healee at or near the area of illness. If physical touching is inappropriate or not permitted, many healers simply stretch out their hands toward the healee and aim the palms of their hands at the afflicted area.

If the healee is not physically present, you may stretch out your hands and with your imagination aim the flow of divine or universal energy toward the person needing healing. Remain in this attitude for a few minutes. You may envision the energy flowing into the healee and picture the troubled area healthy and whole.

This second mode of healing through kything is like intercessory prayer, that is, when we petition God, Christ or one of the saints or holy ones to help a third person. In this setting we want healing or wholeness for someone near to us, perhaps a spouse, a child or a friend who is seriously ill, alcoholic, addicted to drugs, depressed, near exhaustion, losing courage and so on. We may not feel that we have the strength or energy to heal such persons ourselves, and we want to do more than simply be lovingly connected to them. So we pray to God or one of the saints to effect the healing. You may also use kything to deepen this experience. Kythe first with God or the healing figure, then together kythe with the healee.

Famous psychic and spiritual healers describe the state of union they

74

achieve with the healee in images very much like kything. Harry Edwards makes no attempt himself to do anything to the healee but simply to meet him, to be one with him, to unite with him: "The healer then draws 'close' to the patient so that his being is merged, as it were, into that of the patient, so that 'both' are 'one.' "[4] Ambrose Worrall simply said, "I follow a technique I have of 'tuning in,' to become, in a metaphysical sense, one with the patient."[5] Edgar Jackson defined intercessory petition (prayers for a patient's recovery) as a "subject-object bridge."[6]

The special note of the healers in this context is that they are focused on the healee by love, by caring, and by charity. In Agnes Sanford's words, "Only love can generate the healing fire. . . . When we pray in accordance with the law of love, we pray in accordance with the will of God."[7]

3. *Kything as the Transfer of Healing Energy*

If you prefer to perceive spiritual healing as a direct transfer of energy from you to the healee, begin by growing quiet and centered. Then lovingly kythe with the person to be healed, and in that communion *offer the healee whatever energy for healing you may have and express your intention that the healee enjoy fullest health.*

Mietek Wirkus is a gifted healer, a master of a new wave of paranormal healing emerging in Eastern Europe. He arrived in the United States from Poland in 1985 as an advocate of sharing a kind of energy he calls bioenergy to heal the human body.

People tell me about the laying on of hands in their family or church, and how they are healers. It is possible for anyone to help others if there is a positive and caring attitude—provided that

---

[4]Harry Edwards, *Psychic Healing*. London: Spiritualist Press, 1946, p. 26.

[5]Ambrose Worrall and Olga Worrall, *The Miracle Healers*. New York: New American Library, 1968, p. 19.

[6]Edgar Jackson, *Understanding Prayer*. Cleveland: World Pub. Co., 1968, p. 70.

[7]Agnes Sanford, *The Healing Light,* 8th ed. St. Paul: Malcalester Park Pub. Co, 1949.

there is genuine love for others and no trace of rancor, malice or prejudice in the healer. Arrogance, pride, and egoism frustrate healing. Love and genuine kindness raise the energy level: love is the source of healing power.

It is a great joy to help people. You have heard of volunteer blood donors. I am a volunteer energy donor. Humans once had the natural ability to use bio-energy in healing. Our so-called civilization has destroyed these abilities. The time has come to reclaim these inherent gifts.[8]

If the person to be healed is physically present, you may use your hands to touch the healee at or near the afflicted area. Methods for doing this are suggested in the art of Therapeutic Touch developed by Dora Kunz, a spiritual healer, and Dolores Krieger, a registered nurse who has taught the techniques of Therapeutic Touch to thousands of nurses in graduate courses at New York University.

If the healee is not physically present, you may still reach out with your hands and imaginatively touch the afflicted area, sending healing energy to help heal it.

In doing such healing you may experience sensations of heat, tingling, pulsations, etc. in your hand. Many people report such sensations. Their meaning or explanation is discussed in Dolores Krieger's book *The Therapeutic Touch.*[9]

As a general rule all the while these unusual sensations are being felt by you, it is taken as a sign that healing energies are continuing to flow from you into the patient. When these sensations diminish and cease, it is usually taken as a sign that the healee who has been receiving the healing energies is now approaching a state of balance and harmony, at least for the time being. Those who practice Therapeutic Touch and other forms of spiritual

---

[8]Quoted in Milton Friedman, "From Poland With Prana," *New Realities,* July/August 1987, p. 15.

[9]Dolores Krieger, Ph.D., R.N., *The Therapeutic Touch: How To Use Your Hands To Help or Heal.* Englewood Cliffs, NJ: Prentice-Hall, Inc., 1979.

healing also frequently monitor the sensations felt in their hands as a way of diagnosing the balance of energies in the patient's body and of locating problem areas.

While doing a healing kythe you may also feel heat or a variety of sensations in other parts of your body. Sometimes the healee also feels sensations of heat or a change in body temperature, but usually it is only the healer who does. Again, these sensations are interpreted as signs that energy is indeed being transferred from healer to healee.

Kything and Energy

Does kything take energy out of you? Are you drained when you do kything in a healing or supportive role?

These questions presume this last approach toward healing, that is, an energy exchange or transfer. Assuming this framework, the answer to the question is "not usually." The energy that people in kythe normally receive from you will not be noticed by you as a loss, though the *movement* of energy from you or through you is likely to be noticed by you, much as Jesus recognized it when the woman with the flow of blood touched him. When a kythe is entered into consciously, willingly, and lovingly, it seems to energize both parties.

Some of those who believe that it is their own healing energy they share in kythe feel that kything depletes them, since they experience the process as energy being taken from their "own personal supply." Such people need to develop procedures for refilling their personal supply of healing energy.

In contrast, from the viewpoint of "channeling energy" the power that is drawn upon in a healing kythe does not belong to you personally but is a gift of the universe, of God. You may enjoy a special awareness of this energy because you are open to it and prepared to receive it. Provided you remain "open" as you channel it, the healing act should not de-energize you. Quite the opposite, it should allow you to feel your capacity and energy all the more. Channeling healers often speak of themselves being energized by the process.

77

What To Tell the Healee When Kything

People often ask us: "What shall I tell the healee to do while we kythe?" Universally spiritual healers say that healees don't have to do anything special but simply be wherever they are. Healees have no need to intend the healing and no need to formally cooperate with your process.

Of course, many healees would like to participate in the process. If so, you may suggest that they relax, welcome your spiritual presence, and use their imagination to visualize the result they want, e.g., their body thoroughly healed.

If the kything relationship has religious dimensions, you may also invite the healees to become aware of the divine presence by suggesting that they use their creative imagination. "Envision a white light filling your body," you might suggest, or "Feel yourself being surrounded by the Holy Spirit, and see it as a white light."

It is important to remember that kything as such is not primarily a medicinal or therapeutic tool. Nor is it primarily a form of spiritual healing, though sometimes healing does occur during it. First and foremost kything is an act of spiritual presence, a formal affirmation of your oneness with the healee and your loving concern for the healee. Thus, the primary purpose of kything is not lost even if physical healing fails to happen.

For example, you may kythe with people who have suffered a heart attack or stroke, offering them the gift of your presence. In the kythe you present to them in spirit the strength and support of your own health and the healing energies available to them. Your presence is your gift of spiritual support. If someone falls and sprains an ankle, you naturally lend him or her your shoulder for physical support. You don't presume your support will heal the ankle. Similarly, when you kythe you offer the ill person your spiritual shoulder for support.

Generally we suggest that you don't do a healing kythe with someone unless you are asked to, especially if the healee is someone you don't know very well. You may, of course, ask the permission of others to kythe with them for healing. Sometimes they may refuse. The point is to honor the freedom of the other person. Just as God honors your freedom to accept or reject divine love, so you honor another's freedom to accept or reject your healing kythe and gift of unconditional love.

If you would genuinely like to offer your spiritual presence to another in healing and the person is not available to ask permission, and you have a doubt whether or not the person would invite you to do so, offer your healing kythe with the following condition: "This healing kythe is being offered in love. You are free to accept it or reject it."

Summary Steps for a Healing Kythe

Here is a summary set of steps for a healing kythe. Feel free to adapt, modify or enrich the procedure as you see fit:

1. **Get quiet and centered.** Take as much time as you need to accomplish this step since it is the foundation of any successful kythe. It is the first step in entering the realm of spiritual relationship.

2. **Choose to be of service to bring about health and healing in the world.** By making this affirmation, you clearly establish your intention and purpose for entering into a healing kythe.

3. (Optional) **Choose a healing ally or companion and kythe with him or her.** You may choose a religious figure, a symbolic figure, some healing figure, a friend or relative of yours. This step may be used with any of the three healing approaches. It simply introduces another supportive person into the healing kythe. When working with a healing team or group, kythe with the other members of your group before beginning the healing.

4. **Kythe with the person to be healed using the standard three steps—Center, Focus, Connect.** Remember that kything is carried out in a context of unconditional love for the *kything partner*.

5. **Envision the result you want for the person—his or her health and wholeness—and choose it.** Picture the healee in excellent health using his or her body, mind, and spirit in freedom and joy. Then affirm that picture by choosing it, i.e., saying "yes" to it.

6. **Rest in the communion for a few moments or as long as you like.** In the Type I approach only a moment of union is required. The other two approaches usually suggest or require a longer time. If the sense of communion is lost because of distraction or some other reason, gently return to it using imagery and your choice to do so.

7. **You may formally bring the kythe to an end whenever you want.** Apparently, the spiritual connection will remain until you formally close it, even though you go back to your ordinary duties. You may consciously tune in on the union whenever you want, or bring it to an end.

Kything for People in the Healing Professions

A clinical psychologist who began her career as a diagnostic tutor told us:

> In my training as a diagnostic tutor I learned a lot about being a good child psychologist. In tutoring I was taught to begin where the child was—not only where the child was intellectually but also the child's spiritual place, the world which the child's spirit inhabited. It is a different realm from the mind. Going to that place in a child was a way of kything. When I went to the child's spiritual place I would intuitively see a way to proceed with tutoring that would be successful. As a tutor I became very aware when I was present to that spiritual place and when I wasn't. As a therapist I also go to a patient's spiritual place, and I know how valuable kything can be in my work.

If you are a member of a healing profession, you may kythe, as this clinical psychologist did, to be present spirit-to-spirit with any patient you may have, whether it is an emergency or a routine visit, surgery or examination, reporting a bad prognosis or discussing alternatives for future treatment. Kything assures you that you enter the healing relationship with loving care for your patients and their optimal, holistic health.

Kythe with patients using the standard three steps before going into a session of therapy, treatment, examination, diagnosis or surgery.

First, take a few moments to grow quiet and get centered.

Next, hold your patients in loving awareness. Picture the patients in your imagination. See them as very precious to God and their families, and having a unique purpose to fulfill in the world. If you have never seen certain patients or cannot recall what they look like, then hold their names in your mind with a sense of loving and caring. And let yourself want the best for them.

Third, join yourself together with your patient in a caring kythe. Use whatever visual imagery you can to predispose yourself for working spirit-to-spirit with a patient. You may imagine yourselves enveloped in a white healing light or surrounded by God's presence. In that moment of communion—and it need only be a moment—choose to be a healing force in their life. And choose to be guided not only by all the knowledge you have gained through formal study and years of experience but also by your inner movements and the inner wisdom of your spirit.

This process allows you to become spiritually grounded and connected with your patients as you begin your day of professional work.

Kything
and the
Psychological

9. What Kything Is Not

Psychological Growth and Spiritual Growth

Near the beginning of his famous book *The Road Less Traveled,* psychiatrist M. Scott Peck says that he makes no distinction between the mind and the spirit, and therefore no distinction between the process of achieving spiritual growth and achieving mental growth. "They are one and the same," he wrote.[1] Nevertheless, in later sections of the book, Dr. Peck defines terms such as spiritual growth, spiritual goals, and spiritual power in ways that indicate a distinction between those spiritual qualities and mental growth, mental goals and mental power.

Although there is no doubt that spiritual growth and mental growth are processes that are inextricably intertwined in any individual's life, we have found it helpful to emphasize their differences in order to clarify the potential richness of kything activity in both the spiritual and psychological domains.

We have defined kything as a spiritual practice, but it is so only primarily. As is evident to anyone who has experienced kything, it also involves the physical and psychological. In the previous section of the book, Part II, we explored some of the ways that kything impinges on the physical. In this section, we look at kything from the psychological perspective—how it influences the mental and emotional life of those who kythe.

---

[1] M. Scott Peck, *The Road Less Traveled: A New Psychology of Love, Traditional Values and Spiritual Growth.* New York: Simon & Schuster, 1978, p. 11.

What Kything Is

Kything is the practice of spiritual presence, and its purpose is to bring about a loving spiritual connection, union or communion between two or more persons or living things. It is not to be confused with a number of other mental states, spiritual experiences or psychological processes, including: unanimity, consensus, symbiosis, participation mystique, identification, projection, falling in love, empathy, telepathy, mind-reading, channeling, psychological pathology, occult phenomena, a mystic state, a religious experience or an imaginary playmate. We will describe how each of these is different from kything.

Kything is not the same as unanimity or consensus

While kything brings about a spiritual union, unanimity describes the psychological state of two or more people being of one mind. A group of people reach unanimity when all of them think the same thing or hold the same idea, as when all people on the committee unanimously agree that they need to raise money for the church.

Consensus, also a psychological event, occurs when two or more people are of one judgment, that is, when those involved in a decision choose the same thing. Thus, you can say that the church committee has reached consensus when all its members (not just a majority) vote to have a bake sale rather than a raffle to raise money for the church.

Neither unanimity nor consensus demands a spiritual unity among the members who happen to think or choose the same thing. A group of senators or congresspeople can reach unanimity and consensus without kything, and a group of spiritually-minded people can certainly kythe with each other even though they have not reached unanimity or consensus about where or when they will hold their next meeting. In kything, people are simply open and loving toward each other. Recognizing and valuing the uniqueness and preciousness of another is part of the spiritual growth that comes from kything.

Kything is not to be confused with symbiosis

Symbiosis is primarily a psychological state associated with immature ego development. It is a dysfunctional psychological union between two people, usually a mother and a child, though it sometimes happens between spouses or relating adults. Symbiosis is recognized when either of the two cannot differentiate his or her identity from that of the other. Psychologically, in a state of symbiosis the child has never fully separated his or her identity from that of the mother, or the mother has never fully separated her identity from that of the child. In figurative language we often speak of a child being "tied to his mother's apron strings" or we say of the mother, "She has never cut the umbilical cord."

Theoretically, we can imagine two persons who are symbiotically attached being able to kythe with each other, though in reality it is probably more likely that because of their strong dysfunctional psychological union they would find it difficult to differentiate their symbiotic attachment from the spiritual experience of kything. This is because at the unconscious level they already perceive themselves as one and the same being. Kything, on the other hand, is a union that differentiates. The three basic steps of the kything process—get centered, focus on the other, and establish a connection—make this clear. Thus, when you kythe you are fully conscious of who you are, of the uniqueness of the other person, and of your union which is consciously chosen.

Kything is not to be confused with participation mystique

Participation mystique is a term cultural anthropologists use to describe the kind of psychological and spiritual union experienced by members of a primitive tribe. For such people it is as though the tribe—the collective—is the only true living reality, and each of the tribal members exists only by virtue of belonging to the tribe. In a word, it is the tribe which gives them life. Whatever existence they enjoy comes from participating in the life of the tribe. To be cut off from the tribe would be tantamount to death.

Primitive members in a tribal *participation mystique* would certainly be able to be spiritually present to each other. However, because of their psychological union they would probably find it hard to distinguish their tribal oneness from the spiritual experience of kything. Moreover, they would have no reason to make such a distinction.

Kything is not the same as identification

Identification is a natural psychological process whereby I take as my own the beliefs, attitudes, and behaviors of a person I love or respect in order to become like him or her. Normally, identification is a process young people use to help discover their own unique identity. It allows them to identify with different people they admire and respect so they can test whether they would like to become like those other persons. By trying on, in turn, a number of different identities—of their parents, teachers, friends, heros, etc.—they experience a variety of beliefs, attitudes, and behaviors from which they choose or create the way they want to be, and establish their own ego boundaries.

A pathological use of identification occurs when persons are unable to create their own unique set of beliefs, attitudes, and behaviors; instead, they identify, usually unconsciously, with another person, often a parental figure. As a result, they tend to live out the beliefs, attitudes, and behaviors of the other and their true personality or identity is never allowed to emerge.

The process of identification, especially its pathological aspect, has its roots in the very origins of the self. All humans have an incredible need for union, which is activated by the maternal relationship. We all go through life with the longing to re-experience the incredible oneness we knew in the womb with our mother. Sometimes this longed-for union in adulthood is not consciously understood in a healthy way, that is, as a longing for *communion,* a oneness wherein adult individuality and identity is not lost but enhanced. Rather the longing is misinterpreted as a *merging, melting, fusing or dissolving into the other person,* so that one's adult identity is lost. When this occurs, a pathology is set up. The original longing for oneness gets distorted, identification occurs unconsciously, ego boundaries are lost, and the person goes through life looking for someone with whom to merge or into whom to dissolve.

In Jungian language, this person in pathology is not moved by the archetype of *conjunctio,* the energy leading to a relationship of communion, which occurs in kything or love; instead this person is subject to the archetype of the *great mother,* the energy that can swallow or devour one's identity.

On the other hand, when you kythe, consciously connecting spirit-to-spirit with another person, you maintain your own identity (set of beliefs, attitudes, and behaviors) and the person with whom you kythe maintains his or her own identity. In kything, ego boundaries are not lost or broken, but rather they are mutually expanded to embrace the other. In kything, there is no dissolving or melting into each other, but a communion which honors the unique identities of you and the other person.

Kything is not the same as projection

Projection is an unconscious psychological process by which I use others as if they were a movie screen upon which I project some drama going on unconsciously within myself. For example, I may project upon the stranger those undesirable qualities, such as rebellion, revenge, anger or destructiveness, that I cannot accept as a part of myself. Or a man may project upon a woman he finds attractive some feminine qualities in himself, such as gentleness, nurturing, attentiveness or receptivity, that he cannot integrate into his personality or even allow into his consciousness. Projection allows you to put outside yourself (and into someone else) those parts of you that you possess but do not own or integrate. Projection involves attributing to others qualities that you have but of which you are probably unconscious or that you deny. The recipients of your projection may or may not possess the qualities you project on them, for example, the stranger may or may not possess the qualities of rebellion, revenge, anger, and destructiveness to the degree you perceive them in him.

In kything, which is always a consciously initiated process, you do not attribute to others qualities which are really yours. Kything is not a connecting of parts of you to parts of another, but a loving union of two whole realities, spirit-to-spirit. While projection is often an unconscious mechanism designed to separate you from parts of yourself, kything is a free and conscious way of uniting you to others.

Kything is not the same as falling in love

Falling in love is an unconscious process aided by the psychological mechanism of projection. It is usually an intensely emotional and sometimes sexual event by which the lovers experience an extreme and often overwhelming attraction to each other over which they seem to have no control. Because of the mutual projection going on, each sees in the other his or her idealized image of a perfect lover or beloved. Both never want to be out of the other's presence, and feel certain that this intensity of attraction will last forever.

While kything is a consciously chosen act, falling in love seems to take the lovers by surprise. While kything can be started and stopped at will, falling in love seems to have its own schedule. While kything is gentle and spiritual, falling in love is passionate and physical. Nevertheless, we have discovered that lovers tend to be "naturals" at kything.

Kything is not the same as empathy

Empathy is a special skill of the good listener who can say to the other, "I understand what you are going through. I know and accept what you are feeling." To have empathy is to truly understand what another is experiencing and feeling precisely because that individual is the unique individual that he or she is. While empathy is primarily an experience of mental and emotional presence, kything happens primarily on the spiritual level. Of course, some people in kythe have reported experiencing empathy. Although empathy and kything are not the same thing, they share many qualities in common. Both are motivated by openness toward and unconditional regard for the other person. Both reflect the wish to be truly present to the other.

Kything is not just feeling love for someone

Feelings of love for the other person provide an excellent setting for kything, since kything happens in the context of love and openness. We would encourage those who feel love for each other psychologically and emotionally to take one more step and integrate kything into the experience. Use kything to practice being consciously spiritually present to each other.

Kything is not the same as mental telepathy or mind-reading

Telepathy is primarily a method of communication, not communion. It describes a direct, mind-to-mind transfer of knowledge between people without any sensory signals or physical devices. Its intent is to give or obtain information, such as messages, warnings, advice, feelings, and concerns, without using ordinary physical means of communication. Kything is primarily an act of spiritual presence in a context of unconditional loving. While mental telepathy or mind-reading does not necessarily produce kything, people in kythe have reported being able to know certain things going on in the mind and feelings of the other. Have you ever wondered about all those coincidences in your life, like thinking of some people or worrying about them, and soon they telephone you or a letter arrives in the mail from them? It could be that sometimes the spiritual presence produced by kything naturally overflows into an awareness of the psychological and physical concerns of other persons.

Kything is not to be confused with channeling

In channeling, otherwise ordinary people seem to let themselves be taken over by another personality who uses them as a medium or channel for special information and important messages. The most famous of such other-worldly personalities include Seth (channeled through Jane Roberts) and Ramtha (channeled through a woman named J Z Knight). These unusual personalities usually claim to be from some different level of reality, often asserting that they are more highly evolved than people on earth. Much of their communication is of a religious and spiritual nature, encouraging people toward personal and planetary growth. When persons who act as a channel or medium receive these special messages, they are usually in a trance state and their consciousness is frequently taken over by the other personality. Edgar Cayce was probably the most widely known American channel; while in a trance he would diagnose the illnesses of people and prescribe remedies. *A Course in Miracles* is a book that was channeled through Helen Cohn Schucman, a trained psychologist, a professed atheist, and a disbeliever in the paranormal.

In contrast, when you kythe, you are not in a trance state, nor is your identity replaced by the person with whom you kythe. You and your kything partner are in a spirit-to-spirit relationship, each of you present to the other. Kything is not about getting important messages to the world; it is about being spiritually and lovingly present to someone. Although no one but the channel seems able to make contact with an other-worldly entity such as Seth or Ramtha, there are no limitations on those with whom you can kythe. It is a joining of two spirits in love and freedom.

Kything is not an occult phenomenon

Kything is meant to be a very natural and normal activity. There are no magic formulas or superstitions involved. You do not have to be a spiritualist or a medium to kythe. It does not require any unusual spiritual powers. To kythe, all you need is a loving heart and some practice. Anyone, even a child, can learn to kythe. Once you learn to kythe consciously, it feels as normal as walking or talking.

Kything is not psychologically pathological

Kything does not promote delusion, denial or hallucination. It is not a sign of psychosis, neurosis or the avoidance of reality issues such as death, separation, loss, aloneness, etc. In kything, there is no disintegration of identity, loss of ego boundaries or denial of current reality and life experiences. The wish to kythe flows from the basic human desire to be present to someone you love in whatever ways are possible to you. When there is someone you love, you want to be present to that person physically, psychologically, and spiritually. You want not only to be communicating with that person, you want also, if possible, to be in communion with him or her. This wish for close, spirit-to-spirit union is a very natural and healthy desire. Kything is simply a conscious technique that fosters such communion.

Kything is not the same as having an imaginary playmate

When young children are lonely, depressed or fearful, they sometimes spontaneously create a companion to be with them. It is a normal psychological defense mechanism children use to deal with unwelcome emotions. They imagine they have a companion who will protect them, love them, be interested in them, and cheer them up. Parents have found such children happily chatting away with this imaginary playmate, whom the child names and "meets" again and again. Children who are very young would probably find it difficult to differentiate clearly between kything and being with an imaginary playmate.

Kything is different from sacramental Holy Communion

Sacramental Communion uses the physical symbols of bread and wine, and requires eating the sacred bread and drinking the sacred wine in order to effect the communion with Christ. Such Holy Communion happens only during a religious ceremony. Since it is possible to kythe with someone, including Christ, at any time and in any place, kything is much more like a "spiritual communion." Spiritual communion is a spiritual practice that is encouraged when people want to receive the Eucharist but for one reason or another are unable to do so. In spiritual communion, you reverently invite Christ to be spiritually present in your soul. Thus, it is a form of kything with Christ.

Kything is not necessarily a religious experience

While kything is not always a religious experience, it is always a spiritual one. Every human being by nature has a soul or spirit. No one can deny their spiritual nature, though many have denied the reality or usefulness of religion. The realms of the religious and the spiritual sometimes intersect, but there are many experiences of the human spirit that are not necessarily religious, for example, art, music, literature, humor, love, forgiveness, etc. Kything is also one of these. While in Part IV, Kything and the Sacred, we emphasize Christian religious applications and meanings of kything, we would like to point out that kything is not the exclusive property of Christians. Everyone is able to kythe, simply by virtue of having a soul or spirit.

Kything is not the same as a mystical or rapturous state

Kything does not take you into a trance that would be characteristic of the mystical or rapturous state. It is a very centering and conscious experience; it is also down-to-earth and practical. However, some people in kythe have reported profound religious and spiritual experiences during it.

When exploring kything from a psychological perspective it is important to differentiate kything from other phenomena with which it might be confused. That is what we have just done. Now it is important to discuss the way a psychologist might look at and utilize the practice of kything in fostering psychological growth.

10. A Psychologist's Look at Kything

How the Spiritual Can Influence the Psychological

Many psychologists have neglected to look at the possibility that often in therapeutic situations the spiritual level of the person is involved, not merely the psychological. Sometimes clients are touched unconsciously by the therapist's human spirit. As one therapist who was sensitive to her spiritual energies told us:

> When I was still doing my internship as a clinical psychologist, my supervisor told me I had a special ability working with clients in crisis, that they tended to stay with me and get better. She said I had some quality she couldn't name and therapeutic skills that she thought probably couldn't be taught. She resolved her difficulty by calling me a "therapeutic personality."
>
> I began thinking about what she said, to see what I did and if it was teachable.
>
> In my way of thinking, while working with clients I was not only psychologically present to them, I also became spiritually present. On some level I was unconditionally accepting and loving in a way that the other person's spirit knew and was open to it, though we never said so to each other. That's what I think bonded my clients to me so easily and so early. Most people in crisis were especially open, their defenses down, feeling pain and desiring more wholeness. Even though they were in psychological crisis, I believe their spirit could come to a place of peace with

me and entrusted itself to me. I believe the people wanted to come to therapy sessions because of what was happening on a spiritual level.

During crisis sessions I had a sense of being with the client, working from within. I know now that what I was doing was kything, though I didn't have a name for it until now. In the therapeutic relationship, my human spirit and the client's spirit were joined in an effort to bring about emotional stability and healing. I often found myself saying things, not sure why I was saying them, but at the same time aware of the wisdom and right-timing of what I said and did and how it helped the client. Also, I would know inside me somehow when the crisis had passed and their emotions were as stable as possible under the circumstances, so I could bring the session to an end.

I also know now that my supervisor was wrong: What I did can be learned, and I *can* teach others what I did by teaching them how to kythe.

Toward a Psychology of Kything

Strictly speaking, kything as a spiritual practice, like meditation, prayer, and centering, is not in the psychologist's domain. But, then, neither are dieting, jogging and other physical health practices. Nevertheless, psychologists must attempt to make psychological sense out of both the spiritual and physical practices that prove helpful in the therapeutic relationship. Psychologists can make sense out of activities such as kything by finding a place for them within the foundational beliefs they hold about the human psyche.

From a psychological perspective, the following are nine of the foundational beliefs we hold about human life, individually and collectively, that influence our understanding and use of kything within the therapeutic framework.

1. Persons in Relationship

Our first foundational belief is that human persons have a deep need for and a drive toward loving relationship. People need to love and to experience being loved. Moreover, humans feel most alive and complete when they are actively involved in loving. Physically, psychologically, and spiritually, people move toward relating and loving.

Kything is essentially a move toward relating and loving at the deepest of levels. As an Indian guru once put it, "In the beginning only peripheries meet. If the relationship grows intimate, becomes closer, becomes deeper, then by and by centers start meeting. When centers meet it is called love."[1] Kything is a meeting of centers.

2. A Hierarchy of Needs

Our second foundational belief is that people have a hierarchy of needs. The human psyche moves toward nurturing and satisfying these human needs, which have been identified and hierarchized by Abraham Maslow, beginning with physiological needs such as food, shelter, clothing, touch, warmth, etc., then climbing in turn through the levels of safety and security needs, belongingness and loving needs, esteem and self-esteem needs, to the highest level of self-actualization needs such as truth, beauty, humor, unity, religion, altruism, knowledge, etc.

Kything may be used to nurture human needs at all the levels in Maslow's hierarchy.

3. Naturally Oriented Toward Wholeness

Our third foundational belief is that people are naturally oriented toward wholeness. The human psyche never stops trying to find ways to heal its brokenness and its narcissistic wounds. These wounds are some-

---

[1] Bhagwan Shree Rajneesh, *The Way of the White Cloud.* Poona, India: The Rajneesh Foundation, 1975.

times radical ones that make us feel unloved, alienated, frightened, alone, and endangered in the world. The dynamic movement toward healing also applies to ordinary wounds that happen in everyday life such as grief, loss, failure, discouragement, and fear. Most woundedness happens in a context of relationship.

Kything provides a natural dynamic toward healing breaks in relationships. To meet a person at his or her own center, which happens in kything, is to pass through a metanoia (a change of heart) within yourself, because if you want to meet the other person at his or her center you will have to allow that person to reach your center. You will have to become spiritually vulnerable, and kything will eventually teach you how to do that.

Moreover, kything provides the experience of interrelatedness and oneness and, at least potentially, the need to heal the world's woundedness—socially, ecologically, environmentally, politically, etc.

4. Naturally Creative and Powerful

Our fourth foundational belief is that people are by nature meant to shape and create their own lives and make a difference in their world. People are meant to act powerfully and effectively in shaping their own lives instead of simply reacting helplessly and powerlessly to the external and internal "circumstances" of their lives.

At the heart of the creative process is the ability to use the creative imagination to envision the result you want to create, whether it is a painting, a symphony, a new job, a new home, a new relationship, or a college education for yourself or your children. Also essential to the creative process is the ability to choose, or say "yes" to that vision.

In this light, each kything event is a creative act, for you envision the union you want to create and you choose it. Therefore, each time you kythe you are developing your creative skills.

Someone may claim that such activity is just fantasy or wish-fulfillment, but research has shown that Olympic players who utilize visualization and choice of the results they desire perform significantly better than when they do not use these techniques.

5. Self-Actualization and Individuation

Our fifth foundational belief is that humans are by nature called toward the development of their fullest potential, which goal Abraham Maslow has termed "self-actualization" and Carl Jung "individuation."

Under certain conditions, people are able to access more of their own potential. Such conditions include extreme situations of danger and challenge, as when a mother sees her child pinned beneath an automobile and is able to lift the vehicle in order to free her child. It is also possible to release a degree of someone's potential therapeutically through hypnosis, building of self-esteem or ego-development.

Under certain situations, which may be accessed through kything, you can put aside your limiting beliefs about yourself and allow more of your potential to be expressed. The reason this can happen is because, although the ego tends to fear the unknown potential, the spirit knows your true potential and calls you to it.

6. Life Beyond Death

Our sixth foundational belief is that the human spirit inherently believes that its life energy will endure beyond physical death.

A woman tells of her father-in-law who was eighty years old before she met him and who remained in her life for the next sixteen years.

My father-in-law was the first person I ever consciously experienced as loving me unconditionally. I felt really valued and appreciated by him, and I knew, because he told me, that he really liked me and liked being with me. Although he really made a strong impact on my life while he was physically alive, he became more impactful in many areas in the years after his death. Here are some of the ways he continued to make a difference in my life. First, even after his death, the experience of his deep love and valuing of me continued as a part of who I was. I knew that my loving of him, my empathy with his aging and dying, and my sense of spir-

99

itual connection with him was very real and in no way diminished by his death. Second, I knew from him that I also had the capacity to love unconditionally, and I feel his love and connection to me just as strongly, perhaps even more so, today, because my experience of loving unconditionally has deepened and expanded. I am very much able to kythe with him or be connected to his spirit and feel that love whenever I want. Third, his lifestyle of staying vitally connected to nature, curious about science, creative in the arts, attuned to world affairs, and open to loving even until his late 90s was something I wanted for myself.

In kything with him I am in contact with these energies because they were central to his life and he embodied them. When I kythe with him I can choose to perpetuate those energies in myself as I perpetuate my memory and experience of him.

Through kything, you can begin to grasp the enduringness of your own life energy and also the impact you can and do have on others.

7. Fully Conscious and Evolutionary

Our seventh foundational belief is that people are inherently evolutionary, moving toward fuller consciousness and the realization that all elements of creation are interrelated. Evolution of the species has always been present, but now it has reached a level where it needs to be consciously and wisely supported in each individual's journey toward self-actualization and humanity's journey toward world-actualization.

Kything allows you to foster your own self-evolution and to be in touch interiorly with the world's journey toward its own actualization. Kything also offers a way to experience from within the breakdown of ecology, the waste of nature's resources, the needs of those less fortunate. The growing awareness of the state of the planet and of certain individuals on it, achieved through kything with other persons and living things, challenges you to become more and more conscious. Kything is itself a search for oneness and an expression of it.

8. The Integration of Paradox

Our eighth foundational belief is that human consciousness moves toward the integration of paradox. The practice of kything calls upon the human consciousness to integrate in practice a number of paradoxes: When kything, you express the paradox of being in physical space and time yet outside them. When kything with someone you love who is far away, you express the paradox that someone who is absent can still be present. You also enact the paradox of being here physically but somewhere else spiritually. When kything with someone who has physically died, you can transcend the paradox of someone who can be dead yet alive. The practice of kything challenges you to reorganize your categories of reality in ways that go beyond the mere rationally accepted ways of being present to another person.

9. Holistic Development

Our ninth foundational belief is that human development is designed by nature to be holistic. That is to say, healthy human development calls for a parallel and integrated development of body, mind, and spirit.

Today, people do much training and development of their bodies and physical energies, with dieting, workouts, sports, health clinics, and the like. Similarly, they do much training and development of their minds and emotions and the corresponding psychological energies, with education, workshops, reading, therapy, and so on. However, people do little to train and develop their human spirit and its energies. Kything offers a simple way to exercise and develop the human spirit in its ability to be present to itself and to others.

Kything in the Therapeutic Relationship

In the therapeutic relationship the therapist by profession attempts to be as present to the client as possible. As therapist you are present at the *physical* level and attend to the physical needs and physical signals of the client (offering a kleenex or a caring touch, noticing facial expressions and body language). You are also *psychologically* present to the client, attending to the intellectual and emotional content of the interactions, evaluating, reflecting, filling in information, stirring up questions, evoking responses, listening to the tone of voice and other verbal clues the client offers. With kything you have an opportunity also to be *spiritually* present to the client, perhaps even to sense inside yourself some of the internal movements of the client's spirit.

"Because of a kything connection with my clients," reported one therapist, "I find myself asking them, now if they are sad, now if they are angry or anxious, because I feel something like that resonating inside me. Or, when I feel a discontinuity in the session I may ask, 'What's happening?' or 'What are you feeling right now?' Often I find thoughts and insights coming to mind spontaneously—images, remembrances, sometimes stories from my own life—and I usually find some way of checking if the client can relate to them, trusting that they will have some import in the healing work to which the client and I are committed."

Since this therapist knows that both their spirits are aligned with the same goal, that is, to bring about healing and wholeness, she can trust that what comes to the surface of her consciousness is something that will help create the result that both she and the client want. She is not only letting her own spirit and intuition help her therapeutic work, she has through kything also enlisted the spirit of the client to help.

Kything with the client may be done by the therapist alone, by the client alone, or by the therapist and client. There are times when the therapist has been the one conscious of the kything, and times when clients kythe with an unavailable therapist. When client and therapist consciously and formally kythe together before a therapy session, they affirm that their bodies, minds, and spirits are aligned in working together for the same result.

The therapist we quoted earlier told us in greater detail about the way she perceived the therapeutic relationships she often used in crisis counseling:

"I didn't call it kything then. I used to talk about it as 'working from the inside out.' It was clearly a felt experience, I mean I felt it in my body, my gut. The crisis situation rendered both of us open. In light of the intensity and vulnerability of the situation, the barriers between us went down. Often patients would come in beside themselves with anxiety. My first task was to get them centered in themselves, to focus on the crisis and what was happening. I wanted to ground their spirit in what was happening right now. 'Tell me what's going on,' I would say.

"My mind listened attentively and my spirit had a spontaneous loving concern. I was listening from within a communion with the client. I listened not only to the content of the words, but somewhere inside me I was able to feel the gradual quieting and centering of the client's spirit. I could tell there was a part of me monitoring things at another level. I was working at both levels simultaneously. I could watch the process happen from the inner place and I could feel the client growing stable. I would know when we had reached a place where the client was able to function again in a more healthy and in-control way, a sort of inner stability of the spirit. I knew when it was safe to disconnect physically and spiritually.

"As I look back on it, I realize now that the entire counseling session had happened in an altered state of consciousness. I had no concept of the length of time that had gone by. I just knew when a client's spirit was stable and my spirit was centered back in me, so to speak.

"When I disconnected I would silently bless my clients, hoping to seal in their hearts the caring I had shown and also to place them in the hands of God. I wanted their spirit to know that my care and God's care would remain with them, and also that their ego was free to deal with me and the relationship with me, for example, in setting up another appointment or considering some alternatives or suggestions I might offer."

Kything and Internalization

The psychological process called *internalization* is not to be confused with kything. Internalization is a slow, usually indiscriminate and unconscious process of assimilating the behavior and attitudes of someone in your life, usually someone you value or perceive as a model. If you internalized your mother, for example, you slowly and imperceptibly assimilated certain of her behaviors, attitudes, and values. Internalization may be helpful or unhelpful. If your mother treated your health as unimportant and refused to spend money on your health, you may find that you have unconsciously internalized that attitude toward your health by denying its importance and refusing to spend money for physicians.

On the other hand, the internalization process can be helpful and useful. In therapy, many patients learn less dysfunctional ways of living by internalizing their therapists. They see the therapist as a model of how to live and, consciously but mostly unconsciously, they take on the therapist's qualities, attitudes, and possibly even behaviors.

Kything can help transform internalization and make it fully conscious, so that the process of taking into yourself the attitudes and values of another is not indiscriminate or haphazard but clear and motivated. In kything, then, the positive internal change that would happen in you would be freely chosen. If you like what you see in your partner and it seems right for you, you can begin to integrate it into your life. In this, there is no mimicking or role-playing but a conscious choice to live up to your highest potential and claim for your own use the positive energies you identify in another person.

A therapist worked with a young girl who was brain-damaged after a fall down the stairs. When she realized that the child, who had been told she was brain-damaged, equated being brain-damaged with being retarded, the therapist explained what "brain-damaged" meant and how the two states differed. "Even though you may be brain-damaged," she told the child, "you are still gifted." From time to time, the child would phone the therapist and ask her to tell her again how she was gifted. The child was trying consciously to assimilate an understanding of who she was, and to live up to that understanding.

"At that time," explained the therapist, "she didn't know how to kythe with me, so she did the next best thing—she telephoned me. If I had known about kything when I was seeing her, I would have taught her how to use it with me and others for her psychological support."

11. Kything and Psychological Support

Kything for Emotional Support

People often feel lonely, frightened, unloved, overwhelmed, nervous, worried, anxious, and so on. They need emotional support and don't know where to turn. Kything for emotional support is one of the most frequent uses to which kything is put. Here's how to use kything to help.

In kything for emotional support, the first preparatory task is to *decide what positive energy or quality you want, then choose to have it.*

If you are feeling lonely and unloved, the positive energy or quality you want may be someone's loving presence. It is not enough to say, "I don't want to feel lonely or unloved" (though that is probably true). Carry your need beyond what you don't want to what you *do* want. Clarify and choose the positive result you seek from a kything connection. Visualize the positive outcome and say, "I want to feel someone's loving presence near me." Similarly, when seeking a kythe, instead of starting from a negative orientation ("I don't want to feel worried or anxious.") rather start by saying "I want to experience being competent," or comforted, or reassured, or successful or whatever it is you want to experience.

The second preparatory step is to *choose a kything partner who can offer you the quality or energy you desire.*

For example, choose someone who is capable of helping you feel competent, comforted, reassured or successful. The person may be one of your family or friends, a teacher or someone you admire for having that quality. It may be a famous person, living or deceased. It may be a religious figure such as Jesus, one of the saints, Buddha or Muhammad, depending on your theological orientation.

Once you have clarified the positive result you want and chosen a kything partner, establish the kythe using the standard three steps:

1. **Get centered.**
2. **Focus on the kything partner.**
3. **Establish a connection.**

Once the kythe is established:

4. **Create a vision of the positive result you desire.**
5. **In the presence of your kything partner, choose to have that vision.**

There are times when fear, loneliness, and other unwelcome emotions are unavoidable. In this case your kything partner may only be able to offer you strength to endure what must be endured, as when the source of your fear is out of your control, for example, when you are fearful about other drivers being unable to see your car on a foggy night, or when you are concerned about someone else undergoing a serious operation. But, for the most part, you can usually find one or more kything partners whose qualities can help you create the positive results you want.

Before her first day working at a nursing home for dying older people one woman told us she felt very frightened and was sure she would be unable to deal with the nursing home scene.

"I kythed with Mother Teresa," she explained, "and I became very aware of what it felt like to have Mother Teresa's hands and to touch old and dying bodies comfortingly. With Mother Teresa's spirit in me I went confidently to work that first day. And I love my work more than I could have ever imagined. I even say sometimes that I am working in the spirit of Mother Teresa, and people will nod as if they understand. I doubt if they realize how literally I am speaking."

To provide emotional support, you may kythe with your children who are away at school, or a spouse who is away on a trip, or a friend who has moved to another town. We like to recommend that friends kythe with one another when they are apart.

One nursing student at the university missing her boyfriend who was back home in a distant part of the country kythed with him to obtain emotional support. She would hold a photograph of him, play their favorite music on the stereo, and dance around the room in kythe with him. "When I first thought about doing it, it seemed silly," she said. "But when I actually did it I felt his presence very strongly. I do it a lot now. I love the sense of connection to him."

Kythe To Enhance Communication

Kythe before writing a letter to someone you love to create a spiritual and emotional presence. When you receive a letter from someone, kythe with them just before you begin reading it. In this way you read the letter from within a spiritual bond.

You may also kythe with someone before making a phone call to him or her. The person may be someone close to you. On the other hand, the person may be a stranger or someone who could be of important service to you. You can kythe to bring your spirits into mutual harmony or to be open to each other.

Kything To Deal With Loneliness

Lonely persons need a clear outlet for their creativity and for their desire to share life. Some lonely people, sick and confined to their homes, have found an outlet for their loving energies by kything with people in need.

Lonely people can find an inner peace by populating their lives with people to whom they are lovingly connected.

When you are going to a movie alone, instead of just feeling alone kythe with somebody who'd enjoy seeing the movie with you.

When you are feeling alone or missing somebody you love very much, kythe with that person with the intention of feeling his or her presence and love.

After her divorce a woman drove her children to an amusement park for the day. "I felt very lonely," she said. "Most parents were there with their spouses. In fact, when the kids were off on the rides, one man came over to me and said in a surprised voice, 'Are you here all alone?' He made me aware that I was without a loving companion. That reminded me that I could kythe with the people who loved me and would want to be here with me if they knew I would want them here."

A therapist reported that when one of his patients was struggling with a hard decision and felt very alone with it, the patient would kythe with him and feel his support.

Kything in Times of Grief

Use kything as part of the grieving process, not as a way of avoiding grief. Most people after a death, divorce, failure or loss normally tend to avoid dealing with their grief because it is not a comfortable feeling. They would rather not think about it or "get beyond it." The harder they try not to think about it, the more important it becomes. Traditionally, men were accused of being grief-avoiders. There is an old saying, "Women mourn, men replace." Stereotypically, women were seen as usually going through the grieving process, acknowledging what they have lost and are missing. On the other hand, men were seen as tending to replace their wives, children or parents.

Of course, simply to replace is to avoid being in touch with the essence and uniqueness of the person lost. To replace means to deny uniqueness. Those who simply replace are often not in touch with the fact that they are missing someone or trying to avoid pain and grief.

Gretchen realized that her relationship with John was very painful. It was agonizing for the two of them to live in the same house without relating. When John asked for a separation, she was relieved. But she was also sad because she didn't want him to disvalue the twenty years they had lived together. She wished that he would struggle to make the relationship succeed, but she knew he wouldn't. "Twenty years would go right down the drain," she explained. "He would simply walk away and replace me. I knew it. I knew *him.*"

Here is a situation which would probably never get worked out in the physical order. Even though Gretchen wished and hoped she and John could have a conversation and talk things out, she knew there would never be a day on the calendar when they could sit down and talk—and mourn together the loss of a twenty-year marriage relationship. Gretchen's only way to deal with the issue would be on the psychological and spiritual levels. Ideally, she would be able to kythe with John, but she was sure he would not be open to it. Besides, she was still in such pain about the loss that she wasn't sure she could do it either.

What actually happened was she had a dream in which the hoped for conversation happened between her and John. Doing dreamwork with the dream helped her work through a number of the important issues around their divorce, and she was able to perceive John in a new and healthier light. Above all, she was able to mourn the loss.

To mourn or to grieve is to be in touch with the essence and uniqueness of that which is lost and to really know and be in touch with what is missing. It is to say, "I miss having this person by my side to touch and talk to."

To kythe is to actively invite spirit-to-spirit connection with persons no longer physically present. Once you establish that connection, you can do a number of things: you can finish unfinished business; you can say things you wished you had said or done; you can say a good-bye that was never said; you can express how much you miss them; you can express your feelings toward them, the unimportant ones as well as the important ones; you can think and talk about unresolved issues; you can express both sides of your ambivalence; you can make a clear separation (what you were not able to accomplish on the physical level you may be able to accomplish on the spiritual level).

When Stan's mother died he was relieved. No longer would he have to be subject to her "oughts" and "shoulds." No longer would she be trying to run his life. No longer would he have to worry about hurting her feelings by his lifestyle. He did not want her to interfere in his life or try to control him; but it was also true that he loved her and had always wanted her to be happy. "I wanted her to tell me she was proud of me and wanted me to be happy, but she never did. While she was alive she was too caught up in trying to manipulate me." Despite all the disagreement between them, Stan loved his mother and he knew she really loved him. Through kything with his mother Stan was able to deal with some of the unresolved issues and tell her what he felt, especially the most important thing, that they both loved each other.

Also, if you are grieving, kythe with someone who would offer you support through your grief. Kything offers you a chance to choose someone who has gone through the same kind of grief and would help you grow through it and not avoid it. That someone may be thousands of miles away or even someone who has already died. Kythe with someone who can teach you how to deal with grief and give you a healthy perspective.

If you know people who are grieving, you can kythe with them and hold them in your heart; don't protect them from their grief, but support them as they go through it.

If you are dealing with a child or someone else in terminal illness, you may not be able to communicate well face to face (though in many cases it is probably important to make an attempt at doing so). However, you can kythe with the terminally ill person and express what is going on within you and be open to seeing what is happening with the sick person. It has been said that many terminally ill people who are ready to let go of life keep hanging on because they know that their family does not want them to die, and they are trying to please their family or protect it from pain. Though you may not be able to tell sick persons face-to-face that it's okay for them to die, you may be able to do it spirit-to-spirit in a kythe.

Kything for Emotional Release

While kything provides a satisfying way to help release the strong emotion of grief, it also offers a way to deal with the anger, resentment, and hurt that comes from being criticized, misjudged, misunderstood or any other of the many uncomfortable dynamics that happen in relationships.

I was a student counselor at the college and I feared that the Dean of Students was critical of me, that she was suspicious and distrustful of me. At the time, I had no idea how much she was in tune with what I wanted to do at the school, how aligned we were. Sitting near her in chapel one day I kythed with her, sending love and openness. I wanted to be able to be trusting and supportive of her, and I wanted her to feel the same toward me. I wanted our spirits to be at peace with each other and work in harmony for the good of the students.

After the kythe, I noticed a change. She began asking for my help, my opinion, my consultation. She was approaching me, and I found her more approachable. Up to that point, we had only related at the level of communication, not communion. We hadn't been open to each other's spirits, and hadn't realized how much and how easily we could work together for a result we both wanted, the students' welfare.

Of course, you can say that this change in the relationship came about simply because I became more open to her and made myself more available and approachable. That in itself would be a good enough reason to try kything. But I could also feel the change in her behavior. I think it might be what people sometimes refer to as a "change of heart."

With kything, the counselor found a way to initiate openness with the dean. Getting in touch with her spirit and being open to it allowed her to set aside, for the moment at least, certain ego issues and personality differences. As their two spirits joined together that day in the chapel, apparently some of the ego defenses and personality issues became less important, or at least they didn't always remain in the spotlight. Kything allowed them to begin building their relationship at a level deeper than ego.

This starting-with-the-spirit approach may be used with people who are angry at one another, or who have built up mutual resentment, or who are critical of each other.

Kything and Mental Skills

The psychological domain is vast and includes much more than the emotions. Besides using kything for emotional support, you may use it to develop your other psychological capacities and mental skills.

If there is an area in your life where you feel you need to develop your mental capacities and knowledge, find someone who has the qualities you desire and kythe with him or her.

If you are sitting for an examination, defending your dissertation or presenting a report, kythe with someone who has the mental qualities you desire, e.g., clarity, logic, self-confidence, the ability to grasp questions quickly and articulate answers clearly, etc.

When we were preparing a course on the spirituality of Teilhard de Chardin, we kythed with him so that we would be able to truly understand his revolutionary ideas and teach the course from within his spirit.

A college professor told us how she uses kything with her students:

> Before teaching a class, I do what you call kything with my students to be conscious of their needs. I want to be open to the inner voice, to be listening when it speaks. I teach my best when I am open to this voice. When a certain thought just seems to pass through my mind, I treat it as important for somebody in the class and I find a place to put it into my lecture—not always immediately. I may have a sense that this is not the right moment, but if I stay in touch with the inner voice I will sense when the right mo-

ment comes. Then I'll say it. The thought is not necessarily an important insight. It may be just an extra statement or an idea that helps people make a connection between class material and something in their lives.

Over and over, students have come up to me afterward to tell me how important that statement had been for them. I began to realize that the "kything" I was doing connected me to my class at a very special level. It's as though I'm in touch with the needs of the students without even knowing it, and I'm responding with knowledge that they need without consciously and formally "helping" them.

When we asked this professor about her being in communion with the entire class she said, "My object in being in communion, or kything with them is to be open to their intellectual and emotional needs and to respond to them. When I am really teaching well I am totally present to the learners. The only thing that breaks the connection is my ego stuff. When I start wondering whether what I said was indisputably accurate, or start listening to myself critically from the need to 'look good,' it blocks the kything and I am unable to stay fully focused, open, and spontaneous. Sometimes I have to clarify my values to get past my ego needs and stay focused on the result I want for the class. Kything helps me accept the responsibility to teach well, and to stay focused on the larger picture of the dynamic, interactive learning that happens mutually, moment to moment."

Kything with Writers, Artists, and Composers

You may kythe with a person whose artistic skills you would like to develop. Jean Houston, who has mentioned kything in her books and teaches it in her workshops, used to show budding art students how to commune with famous artists and teachers, so that the young students would be open to the skills and energies of the masters—with startling results!

113

Educator George Leonard in *The Silent Pulse* described an aikido student who used spiritual presence to embody an old aikido master. When the young student performed, said Leonard, the room was perceptibly filled with the old master's energy.

A professor of creative writing assigned his students the task to write one short story in the style of J.D. Salinger and another in the style of Flannery O'Connor. To Renee, one of the students in his class, these were two of her favorite authors. So she kythed with each of them and wrote from within the spiritual connection. The process proved so successful that the professor was stunned at how like Salinger and O'Connor Renee's stories were.

We know that kything, which is a spiritual activity, can have effects on the psychological level. We still don't understand the spiritual dynamics that are going on. It's as if one spirit says to another spirit, as this young woman apparently did to Flannery O'Connor's and J.D. Salinger's spirits in kythe, "I want to know you well enough to do what you do, to write as you do." Perhaps there is some kind of alignment of minds as well as spirits that occurs, or the sharing of a spiritual energy such as creativity.

Musicians may kythe with the composer of the music they are performing, to feel the spirit, movement, tempo, and mood of the music as the composer did. One conductor claimed that he had a sense of Beethoven's presence and could tell whether or not the tempo and manner in which he conducted a Beethoven piece met with that ancient master's approval.

Drama students are always being asked to get into the mind and spirit of the character they are playing on stage. When we describe kything to actors and actresses many say it is very similar to what they do when they assume a role. If the character being portrayed is an historical reality, kything seems quite possible. But what of a fictional character? There seems to be no human spirit with which to kythe, unless it is the spirit of the character's creator, the author of the play.

When studying or reading, kythe with the author(s) of the text. You may presume they would want you to share their knowledge and interest in the material, whether it be academic, biography or fiction.

Kything and Consciousness

To kythe is to initiate an act of conscious awareness at the level of spirit. Consciousness is more than awareness. It is *awareness plus appropriate action.* When you kythe with a partner, don't just ask for support and wander off. Take appropriate action. Look for places you can practice the attitudes and behaviors you invited or wanted from your kything partner. Through kything you become conscious that you have alternative ways of behaving, thinking, and responding. Begin to take appropriate steps to develop your potential and expand yourself.

Communication and Communion

Kything is essentially a relational event, and its objectives always include the establishing of loving communion at the spirit-to-spirit level. As a spiritual act kything establishes spiritual presence and by nature fosters interpersonal closeness and interpersonal growth.

But communication is a relational event, too. And it may be important to highlight their differences. The differences between communication and communion are often hard to see, but they are there. For example, how often have you seen couples who don't get along or can't communicate with each other but who still love one another, or parents and children who disagree, argue, threaten each other, and often stop seeing each other or communicating, yet still profess to love one another, and do. Love, which exists and operates on a spiritual dimension, is distinguishably different from the psychological ability to communicate and get along.

Just as there are many levels of communication such as friendly chatting, teaching, business discussions, and therapeutic interactions, so there are many levels of communion such as simple momentary spiritual presence, a married couple who have enjoyed a lifelong spiritual bond, a community joined in worship, and the supernatural network of the communion of saints.

Just as there are many reasons for communicating, such as bringing information, giving instruction, sharing experiences, telling stories, expressing feelings, looking for ideas, making plans, resolving conflicts, etc., so there are many reasons for communion, such as connecting spirit-to-spirit over time and space, providing spiritual support and nurturance, praying, healing, grieving, sharing, loving, tapping into spiritual energies, establishing a sense of oneness, etc.

For animals, spiritual presence is a familiar factor throughout their lives, often even at the level of community. Seals, whales, salmon, herring, and alewife fish are only a few of the species who return to their homes to spawn together, often monogamously. At mating season the Galapagos turtles return to their special island to breed, no matter how many thousands of miles away they may have wandered in the meantime. A homing instinct is the usual explanation for these phenomena, but the instinct theory leaves much to be explained. Perhaps the animals enjoy an unconscious communion that moves them to find their homes and mates.

Primitive people apparently had ways of being spiritually connected to each other in the tribe. They learned to know if someone's spirit was lost, sad, sick or in trouble. Communing was probably a spontaneously-developed skill in those eras. (It has always been especially noted between mothers and their children.) In time, the unconscious communion of primitives evolved into communication. But somehow in learning how to communicate, civilized folk forgot how to commune. And now after inventing sophisticated communication systems, we are being called to develop *conscious communion*—not to replace communication but to enhance it and fulfill it or, in other words, consciously to root communication in its true foundation, communion. In this context, communion is seen to contain communication, and communication is seen as leading toward communion. As a therapist explained to us:

> It happens with some of my clients. They have integrated communication and communion. They feel a need—or a wish—to stay connected to me during the time between sessions. And they often call upon this connection to ask themselves, "What would Ann say if I told her about this situation?" and find themselves "hearing" what I might say. It's not like me telling them

116

what to do. It's as though they are experiencing the same process that would occur in a therapy session with me. They hear the kinds of questions I would probably ask to help them sort out things. They feel connected to me, yet remain free to explore their thoughts and make any choices they need to make. We stay in a relationship in which there is communion and communication.

Interestingly, what they often hear and later relate to me is me at my therapeutic best, the essence of my professional wisdom, a true example of communion, and a communication I would have wanted to make.

12. Kything and Love

Love and Will

For M. Scott Peck, love is closely related to the disciplines and practices that help bring about spiritual and psychological growth. In fact, he says, love provides the energy and motivation behind the discipline we must exercise in order to pursue our mental and spiritual growth. Unlike many other psychiatrists and psychologists who would define love primarily as an affective experience, Peck defines love in evolutionary terms as "the will to extend one's self for the purpose of nurturing one's own spiritual growth or another's spiritual growth."[1]

For Peck, then, love is primarily volitional rather than emotional, an action more than a feeling. Love is an act of the spirit, or will, expressed in conscious ego choices, and it calls for effort, patience, and discipline. To be love it must be of sufficient intensity to translate itself into action. As Saint Ignatius observed in his Contemplation for Obtaining Divine Love in the *Spiritual Exercises,* "Love is shown more in deeds than in words."

Thus, for Peck, "falling in love," because it is primarily an overwhelmingly powerful feeling and not a free and conscious choice, is not an act of love; nor is sexual lovemaking in itself necessarily an act of love. Love, as he understands it, is not restricted to the self or, as in "falling in love," to one other person. For Peck, love does not stop with the beloved but continues to extend itself to more and more others. How can I be satisfied with

---

[1] M. Scott Peck, *The Road Less Traveled.* New York: Simon & Schuster, 1978, p. 8.

118

reaching out to just one other person to help nurture his or her spiritual growth? If I truly love myself and another, will I not naturally reach out to another and another and yet another, nurturing their spiritual growth, helping them evolve? Love is an act of evolution, that is, in loving you extend your limits and boundaries in a process of self-evolution, but because love is interpersonal you are also encouraging others toward self-evolution and the stretching of the boundaries of their selves.

One of our kything students described kything as loving in a way that reminded us of Peck's definition:

> I am learning to use my ability to be spiritually present and connected to others in many different ways. I like to think of what I do when I kythe as offering ultimate hospitality to someone I love. I openly invite them to enter my very life and being in a heart-to-heart experience. And when they in turn offer me the freedom to do likewise with them, it feels like a wonderfully expansive way to celebrate life and relationship!

Scott Peck presents a glowing description of the person who has been loving (according to his definition) for many years. In it, he paints a picture of spiritual growth that "can be achieved only through the persistent exercise of real love."[2]

> What transpires then in the course of many years of loving, of extending our limits for our cathexes, is a gradual but progressive enlargement of the self, an incorporation within of the world without, and a growth, a stretching and a thinning of our ego boundaries. In this way the more and longer we extend ourselves, the more we love, the more blurred becomes the distinction between the self and the world. We become identified with the world. And as our own ego boundaries become blurred and thinned, we begin more and more to experience the same sort of feeling of ec-

---

[2] *Ibid.,* p. 97.

stasy that we have when our ego boundaries partially collapse and we "fall in love." Only, instead of having merged temporarily and unrealistically with a single beloved object, we have merged realistically and more permanently with much of the world.[3]

Cathecting, a term coined by Sigmund Freud, is the psychological process by which a person or object becomes important to you. Once cathected, this person or object is invested with your energy as if it had become a part of yourself and you had given life to it within you; when this happens the relationship between you and the other person or object is called a *cathexis.* True love requires an emotional cathexis to initiate it, because we can only love that which is somehow emotionally important to us. But if we say that love itself is merely a feeling, we confuse loving with cathecting, the psychological process that initiated the loving. Kything too is a loving action and may require cathexis to motivate and initiate it, but it is not to be confused with cathecting any more than you would confuse an advertisement that led you to buy a product with the product itself.

To kythe with more and more people is to extend the boundaries of your self and to expand and develop your loving nature. You may begin by loving the person you want to marry and expand your boundaries to love (i.e., to nurture the spiritual growth of) the other members of your spouse's family. Similarly, you can love the friends, colleagues, students, clients, patients, group members with whom you deal, and in this way you expand the boundaries of your self even more. In Peck's metaphor, as you extend yourself to nurture the spiritual growth of more and more others, it is as if your soul grows fuller and fuller with those you love and the skin of your soul becomes stretched and thinned making it easier for you to love and to be touched at the center of your being.

Kything is an exercise of the "will to extend oneself," that is, to love. The aim of kything is also always spiritual growth of self and others. In light of Peck's definition of love, kything may be viewed as a practice of true love.

---

[3] *Ibid.,* p. 95.

As you meet the spirits, or centers, of more and more beings through kything and other ways of loving, it may happen, in Peck's words, that your "own ego boundaries become blurred and thinned," but this is not because you are losing your true identity. Quite the opposite, it is because you are beginning to be present to and interconnected, spirit-to-spirit, with much of the world.

When you kythe with someone in deep loving, your identity and the center of your being is not lost, but strengthened. As the French Jesuit priest Teilhard de Chardin explained it, "True union, that is, spiritual union or union in synthesis, differentiates the elements it brings together. This is no paradox, but the law of all experience. Two beings never love one another with a more vivid consciousness of who they are as individuals than when each is in communion with the other."[4]

Attention and Presence

For Peck, the principal work of love is to give *attention.*[5] The principal act of kything is to establish *presence,* mutual spirit-to-spirit presence. A major quality of psychological and spiritual presence is attention. Psychologically and spiritually, a lack of attention implies a lack of presence. Although I can be physically present to you without being attentive to you, I cannot be psychologically present to you and at the same time be inattentive. To withdraw my mental or emotional attention from you is to withdraw my psychological presence from you.

Kything, as an expression of loving, allows you to enlarge your self beyond the boundaries of your embodiedness. Ultimately, both loving and kything are designed to help you transcend your limits and become consciously and spiritually one with the cosmos. The process of getting to that level of maximum consciousness is the challenging and rewarding work of spiritual growth. It is the work of a lifetime.

---

[4]Pierre Teilhard de Chardin, *How I Believe.* New York: Harper & Row, 1969, p. 54.
[5]M. Scott Peck, *op. cit.,* p. 287.

Spiritual Growth and the Evolution of Consciousness

Spiritual growth may be measured by one's growth in or evolution of consciousness. For Peck, spiritual growth implies spiritual power, which is the capacity to make decisions in greater and greater consciousness, ultimately to make decisions with total awareness.

Thus, love may be defined as the will to extend yourself in order to help yourself and others make choices and act with ever greater awareness. Would this not also be a description of the role of the health professional and the spiritual healer?

Consciousness of the Heart

Current brain research at the National Institute of Mental Health (NIMH) has revealed something that has been known by many cultures, something that the NIMH calls the "conversation between the brain and the heart." In more technical language, the researchers say, there are unmediated nerve connections between the heart and the limbic structure, the metaphoric, symbolic functioning part of the brain that fosters bonding, specifically mother-child bonding. This midbrain area collates information from the external world with what may be called "intuitive information" coming from non-sensory sources. The midbrain sends that information to the heart instant by instant. The midbrain then receives instructions from the heart as to the response to make to the world out there. This is the conversation between the brain and the heart. How you relate to the world is influenced by this connection and conversation.[6]

To what "heart" is the NIMH referring? According to Joseph Chilton Pearce, who summarized the research, it is our physical heart as well as our "subtle or spiritual heart." In his own words:

Our physical pumping heart is the translating mechanism for consciousness, and the subtle heart is the generative force itself. The

[6]Joseph Chilton Pearce, "The Art of Mothering," *Mothering*, Spring 1985, p. 20.

heart is the translating mechanism. The heart translates and sends its signals to the brain of a real, underlying conscious response to the world out there. This is earthshaking news![7]

During the fifth to the ninth months in the mother's womb the infant bonds, or imprints, to the mother's heart. This genetic encoding requires that the infant be returned to that immediate proximity with the mother's heart immediately after birth. Bonding occurs when the child is given back to the mother for skin-to-skin contact. According to Joseph Chilton Pearce, author of *The Magical Child,* "All mothers from time immemorial put their babies to their left breast at birth because that puts the child's heart in proximity with the mother's heart."[8]

Pearce claims that traditional hospital childbirth has disrupted bonding at birth in most cases. As a result of that initial disruption of the bonding process, the ongoing series of bondings between the child and mother and between the child and society are impaired.

Pearce's research underlines the tremendous importance of bonding, of a heart-to-heart union that begins long before an infant breathes. Kything in love keeps us aware that the need for bonding at all levels of human life—body, mind, spirit—is primary and pervasive.

Kything and a Loving Bond

By its very definition, kything is a loving presence. Love may be expressed on many levels of human life—words, thought, intentions, feelings, actions, etc. But love in its fullest sense leads to union, it creates a freely-established bond between you and the object of your love. In simple language, you want to be near or present to the object of your love.

Just as the physical body longs to be touched by another person, and the human mind longs to have communication with another human person, to be listened to and understood, so the soul or spirit longs for com-

[7] *Ibid.*
[8] *Ibid.,* p. 21.

munion, to be in spirit-to-spirit union with others. If, as some say, the core wish of every human person is to be bonded in love to other human beings, then we can say that the spirit is always disposed for kything.

If the primal unconscious experience of the fetus in the womb is of symbiosis, that is, of sharing the very same life as the mother, then kything becomes a way consciously to transform and expand that primal symbiotic experience. In primal symbiosis the infant does not have an ego with which to choose to be in relationship, so the symbiotic relationship is one of unconscious identification, i.e., the infant perceives itself as being the same thing as the other person or of being a part of the other person. In contrast, when kything you use your ego's choice power to enter into and stay in spirit-to-spirit relationship to those people whom you love.

Because the kything relationship is conscious, freely entered into, and freely terminated, it transcends the unconscious symbiosis of the infant yet allows the fulfillment of the human core wish to be bonded in love to another and to many others.

If the opposite of love is not hate, but fear, as asserted by psychiatrist Jerry Jampolsky and many others, then kything helps break down the barriers of fear and distrust that underlie so many of our individual and world problems in relationship.

Kything in Love To Relate to Groups

One lecturer dealing with the fear of criticism said,

I used to see my audience just waiting to be critical of me. The truth of the matter was they were open to me but I wasn't open to them. Kything allowed me to connect lovingly with my audience and see how truly open they were and how eager to hear what I had to say. They had paid their money to hear me, not to criticize me. So now, while everyone is getting seated and calming down for my lecture, I may look as though I'm just sitting there waiting for things to begin. But I'm actually kything with all of them, sending my love to them, opening my heart and asking their hearts to be open to me and what I have to say.

In most cases, his audience is probably not aware that their spirits are being touched. Some may even have blocks or barriers to receiving the love and openness he is projecting. But overall, he is creating a general atmosphere of love and openness in the group and aligning the group's energies. This often breaks down the barriers of the resistant others helping them get caught up in the spirit of the group.

To kythe in such a setting, as a lecturer or speaker: (1) grow quiet and get centered, (2) focus on the audience and the result you want for the session (it may be love and openness, sharing and learning, being a channel for healing and growth, etc.), (3) establish connection and affirm it. It is also important after the class or lecture to (4) break the formal kything connection. You may do this simply by saying aloud, "This is the end. Thank you," or by giving them a wish or a blessing such as, "I hope you will integrate into your lives the growth and insight that has happened here today." You may also break the kythe privately with some short ritual action like washing your hands or taking off your jacket or by getting recentered in yourself.

The reason for breaking the kythe is that the audience has been used to receiving energy and insight from you. Closing down the kythe simply says that the directing-of-energy structure is no longer in effect. It's like turning off the water faucet when you've finished with it. You turn off the kythe when the sharing of presence is over.

Coinherence Kything

There is a very special way of kything called coinherence kything, which is appropriate for those who share a loving bond with each other. It describes a form of presence that involves a conscious awareness of the physical bodies of the two persons in kythe. Usually, during the third kything step, you're asked to imagine you and the other person as connected or joined. In coinherence kything you're asked to *image your two bodies coinhering,* so that I experience your mouth and my mouth as one mouth, your throat and my throat as one throat, your lungs and my lungs as one set of lungs, your hands and feet and my hands and feet as one set of hands and feet. In this way, you picture you and me coinhering body within body—becoming one—so that if you were to utter a prayer it would feel as though both of us were uttering that prayer using the same mouth, throat, breath, and voice.

At this step of joining, your imagination pictures not merely a touching of souls or hearts, but of your head filling the space of my head, your body superimposed on my body, so that your fingers are not only your fingers but mine as well. And, ideally, your mind is pictured not only as yours but mine as well.

Obviously this coinherence is initiated only at the imaginal level; there is no commingling of our skin and bones nor any fusion of our bodies, even at a cellular level. The Biodance may be startling, but it is not *that* startling. The imagination can picture it even when such a union may not be physically possible. The union is a spiritual one, although those who have tried it have observed that it may be quite palpably felt.

The purpose of the coinherence kythe is primarily to enhance the experience of compassion, which literally means "an ability to feel or experience along with someone else." For example, you might do a coinherence kythe with a sick friend to be able to enter more fully into their suffering. As one woman said to her sick friend as she was initiating a coinherence kythe, "I want to feel for a few minutes what it would be like to live in your skin, to be in your body; and what it would be like to have you live inside me. And I also hope that when we kythe you will be able to feel what it would be like to live inside me and have me living inside you."

When you kythe with your spouse or a beloved friend, you may choose to use a coinherence kythe from time to time. Coinherence is often most powerful for those deeply in love, and may be used especially effectively when the couple are not physically present to each other. As one man told us, "When I go walking in the woods when my wife is away, I take her with me in kythe. Since she is much more attuned to nature than I am, I usually coinhere in her so I can experience the trees and the brook or the things along the path with her senses and enjoy the intensity of her appreciation.

When I do this, I not only delight in the forms, smells, and sounds around me, I feel her presence within me. At those times I feel more at one with her than at almost any other time." In coinherence, your intent is principally to deepen the experience of union and foster compassion—to feel how the other feels.

Kything for Enjoyment

Sometimes you want to express joy, to release the overflow of wonderfully positive emotions that you're feeling. Kything can help this release.

How often do you want to be with certain people just because they are fun to be with and they let you feel like a happy kid again? Most of us, given the choice, would prefer to spend our lives enjoyably.

We encourage you to kythe with people who are a delight in your life.

If you are sitting in the same room with someone you like, kythe with him or her. Enjoy the fact that you are spiritually joined as well as physically and mentally present.

If someone you enjoy is absent, kythe with that person, especially if you are doing something you think he or she would enjoy—eating, relaxing, taking a walk, looking at scenery, enjoying art, listening to music, etc. To fully enjoy the kything try a *coinherence kythe.*

Picture your tongue and teeth merging so that you could enjoy the taste of something with the other's tongue and teeth as well as your own. Also imagine letting your bodies coinhere so that if you are swimming in the ocean, for instance, your partner feels the sensations of the water as well as you. In your imagination you can even join your minds and emotions so that you are sharing the feelings of both of you.

Notice that in coinherence kything you do not lose your identity; rather you double your enjoyment by connecting with your kything partner. You experience the two of you experiencing something joyful.

Think of all the situations where you might coinhere with a friend such as when you are at a movie, a jazz concert or a county fair.

Dancing with a partner while in a coinherence kythe is a very special experience, for you can feel the dancing movement from within yourself or from within your partner. In this way, you discover the wonderful versatility of the spirit and its ability to experience union in many forms. Coinherence kything with someone you deeply love is a powerful experience of presence.

The Ministry of Presence

A hospital chaplain in residency training told us that she had developed what she called a ministry of presence.

When she had first been sent into a hospital setting, she was expected to visit rooms and pray with the patients there. But to walk in and announce to someone, "I have come here to pray with you," was not natural to her, especially when she didn't know the patients personally. Besides, she explained, she wasn't always comfortable reciting formal and traditional prayers. That's how she began to evolve her ministry of presence.

In this process, she would stop for a few moments to get centered before she entered a person's room. Upon entering, she would approach the person, quietly sending love from her heart. Then, as she described it, she would be "present spirit-to-spirit." Making such a connection felt natural and appropriate to her. From this communion she would gain a sense of how best to be with the person.

Often, I would just stand or sit silently in the presence of the person, holding her hand or touching her gently or simply being near. In that loving presence I would continue praying in my heart until I felt an inner movement to speak or to take my leave—whatever felt most right.

If I chose to speak, I would say whatever came to mind. For example, I might mention my prayer intentions or my inner thoughts. If the person seemed open to it, I might invite her to pray aloud with me, however she wished. At other times, I might say something pleasant or enjoyable that occurred to me, comments that might be interesting or comforting.

But sometimes the person was not awake or conscious, or it

just seemed right not to speak aloud at all. At those times I was equally comfortable simply sharing my loving presence in silence.

When we mentioned kything to her, she said it described what she was doing with hospital patients. She liked our term "kything" and we liked her expression "ministry of presence." In a very true sense, kything is a ministry of presence.

The young chaplain suggested one of many possible ways to develop a ministry of presence. Our guess is that many others have found their own way to a similar ministry based on love and mutual spiritual presence. For example, kything with infants, those who are brain-damaged, and the very elderly, where there might not be much communication possible, naturally invites communion.

Kything With Older People

If you are well into middle age and would like to live into old age lovingly, consciously, wisely, creatively, and with good humor, find someone who continually, in Scott Peck's definition, "extends one's self for the purpose of nurturing one's own spiritual growth or another's spiritual growth." Let such a person be a model for you and kythe with him or her. One woman found just such a model in her neighbor.

Mrs. Roberts started tennis at 60 and took up yoga at 70 years old. She was also a weaver. She started with raw wool, carded it, dyed it, spun it, and then wove it or knitted with it. She was also a bird-watcher and took long walks every day into her late 80's. To me she was an example of a creative, healthy, wise, curious, gracious, and high-spirited older person. She was a great model. To kythe with her was to know her on a spiritual level. I enjoyed letting my spirit know her spirit and be a model for me. In her I could see that instead of fearing old age I could look forward to living it gracefully and dynamically.

Kything
and the
Spiritual

13. Kything and Spiritual Energies

Spiritual Energies

According to a story told by Martin Buber, Rabbi Mendel once boasted to his teacher Rabbi Elimelekh that on evenings he had seen the angel who rolls away light before the darkness, and at morning the angel who rolls away the darkness before the light. "Yes," said Rabbi Elimelekh, "in my youth I saw that too. Later on you don't see these things anymore."

As we grow out of the idealism of youth our spiritual energies, like those of Rabbi Elimelekh, seem to be among the least utilized of our human faculties. Growing into adulthood, we tend to live on the surface of life and at times to put our highest value on appearance. "We have concentrated on the successful appearance of things," wrote Jean Houston sadly, "to the starvation of the roots of who we are."[1] The spiritual is often the first level of living to be dropped or forgotten, and yet it deals with the core of our life and meaning, the roots of who we are.

When asked about the spiritual domain of their lives, most people hardly know how to talk about it. When asked if they can differentiate the spiritual from the religious or the spiritual from the psychological, they find it difficult to do so.

Although body, mind, and spirit are inextricably intertwined in the fabric of life, it is possible to point to threads of experience that are primarily physical, others that are primarily psychological, and still others that are primarily spiritual. While most people associate human feelings

---

[1] Jean Houston, "The Arts of Acknowledgement," *AHP Newsletter,* March 1979, p. 8.

133

with the psychological dimension of life, it is clear that humans have at least three distinguishable levels of feelings. First, the body has its own set of *physical feelings:* those the body feels after a hard workout with exercise equipment, after a hot shower, after a large meal, after sex, etc. Second, the mind and emotions have their own set of *psychological feelings:* delight at solving a mathematical problem, anger after being manipulated, joy at seeing someone you love after a long absence, grief at someone's death, etc. Third, the human spirit has its own distinguishable set of *spiritual feelings:* peace after forgiving someone, a sense of creativity, an awareness of having made a commitment, a sense of truth in having an insight, a sense of courage in standing up for one of your rights, etc.

In a similar way, we can show how the body, mind, and spirit each has different sets of *wants and desires.* Begin by developing a list of desires your body has: to feel rested, to touch, to experience pleasure, to be well-fed, etc. You can compile another list of desires for your mind: to think, to compare, to deduce, to imagine, to remember, etc. Still other experiences qualify as desires of the spirit or soul: to be in touch with your life's purpose and meaning, to be able to discern your true path, to have the courage to do what you know is highest and truest for you, to be able to perceive the unity of all life, to feel the energy of transmitting life and enjoyment to others, to enjoy aesthetic pleasure, to have wisdom, to know yourself with your limitations and potentials, to have the energy to carry out the decisions you make, to have compassion for yourself and others, to be of service to others, to be open to the inner movements of your spirit, to have the courage to face your failures and fears, to believe in yourself and trust in your essential goodness, to be able to create the life you really want, to live your life in fulfilling and creative ways, to have a zest for life that reaches to the core of your being.

Kything, primarily a spiritual activity, responds especially well to such spiritual desires and needs because it is open to spiritual energies. In the following sections we will suggest kything exercises around seven basic kinds of spiritual energy.[2] Although there are probably many other kinds of spiritual energies, these seven are central to living a full human life. They are:

(1) *bearing life and transmitting life at* all levels of being;

(2) *self-awareness and self-affirmation,* the ability to know and affirm the truth of who you are;

(3) *courage* and its related energy, forgiveness;

(4) *compassion,* or the ability to feel and express unconditional love;

(5) *commitment,* or the ability to make choices and to carry them out;

(6) *wisdom, discernment,* the ability to discriminate and give names to things, plus other spiritual energies related to intelligence;

(7) *cosmic-consciousness,* the unitive experience, the ability to see yourself and the world from God's point of view, or at least from a transcendent perspective.

Kything and Transmitting Life

In its most basic sense, *transmitting life* is an expression of creativity; it refers to bringing something new into the world, whether it is a human child, a work of art, a new recipe, new knowledge, a new project, a new relationship, or something else that you have never produced before. Kything transmits life first of all by creating a spiritual relationship that can share energies and love in and through its union. In kything, you may release those energies for yourself or others in order to create works of art, new projects, new relationships, etc.

Who are the people who possess this spiritual energy to transmit life? You probably recall having teachers somewhere along your educational path who made the subject matter they taught really exciting. When they

---

[2]These energies are discussed in more detail in our book *Prayerways.* New York: Harper & Row, 1980, pp. 10–12.

stood up in front of a classroom energy was flowing out of them and it came through in their actions and in the words they spoke. To be in their class wasn't boring or tiring. Quite the opposite. When they taught, you felt alert, alive, challenged, functioning at your best. For such a dynamic teacher you probably didn't even mind doing homework most of the time.

"I remember my high school biology teacher," recalled one woman. "I never dreamed I could be excited about memorizing parts of nervous systems and looking through a microscope, but remembering it today I can still feel the sense of energy he exuded. It wasn't a personal relationship with the teacher; I mean, I wasn't sexually attracted. His teaching was simply full of life. When you were in that class it was exciting."

"I remember a team of workshop leaders who taught hypnotherapy to professional therapists," recalled a clinical psychologist. "When I get in touch with those few days I spent in that seminar, my mind lights up, my imagery is in full color. The instructors were bursting with life, I understood the truth of what they were saying, the class was positively electric, and I couldn't wait to begin exploring the new ideas."

On the other hand you certainly had teachers who were unquestionably intelligent and clear but who lacked the spiritual energy of transmitting life.

"I was totally bored with chemistry," explained the same woman who liked biology. "The teacher was clear and knew his subject inside and out, but there was no love or excitement in his class. I guess his spirit just wasn't there, and it certainly didn't touch mine."

While the chemistry teacher's *mind* communicated the facts of chemistry clearly, orderly, and intelligently, the biology teacher did that and more: his *spirit* was transmitting life—with the flavor of biology.

In our language, the biology teacher had created a kind of spiritual presence with his students. He knew that humans are naturally drawn into relationship. It's a need as basic as eating and sleeping. People are by nature relating beings. The members of his biology class were spirits joined together with a single focus, a group of people exploring life together, looking at the world through the lens of biology. This kind of spiritual union found in special classrooms often provides the groundwork for creative discovery in science and research.

136

Spiritual Energy and Special Others

At the root of your best creative work is probably a relationship with a special teacher or mentor who had the spiritual energy to transmit life to you. Recall that person who triggered in you the energy to transmit life and kythe with him or her when you are in need of this energy.

We tend to picture a concert pianist as a solitary artist practicing and performing as if no one else existed. But often there has been another person with the spiritual energy to transmit life who passed on to that pianist the love for making music. Perhaps today for this pianist the mere sight of a piano triggers this love for music and the desire to transmit life through it, but early on there was probably someone who touched off the spark. Seldom does an artist—or any other creative person—come into the professional world without having encountered someone who called forth that spiritual spark.

Let your creativity be sparked by another's creative energy, in order to go beyond your current limits to create something new in the world, perhaps many new things. In kything with great creative spirits you can learn about your own potential. In seeing what someone else has done, you can begin trying to do things like that, using the creative person's spirit as a model and an inspiration. Kythe with them as a stepping-off place, and go beyond them. This is what it means to be "inspired by" someone: to be *in* his or her spirit, to be in kythe.

14. Kything, Self-Affirmation, Courage, and Forgiveness

Self-Affirmation and Self-Esteem

The second area of spiritual energies on our list of seven focuses on *self-awareness and self-affirmation.* Today's popular word for it is self-esteem. Self-esteem is probably more a spiritual quality than a psychological one, even though many psychologists deal with it. It reveals fundamental characteristics of who I am and how I go about my life and work. Self-esteem is about my essence and in many ways describes my life-stance: I see myself as worthwhile and live confidently or, on the other extreme, I see myself as inadequate and live in fear. As a spiritual energy, self-awareness and self-affirmation can be developed through kything.

Self-esteem is a product of realistic self-awareness and self-affirmation, which are in turn based on the more fundamental spiritual energy of truth. In this chapter we focus on self-awareness, self-affirmation, and self-esteem, since they pose the concretely practical question: "What is the truth about me?" Self-awareness asks that question, self-affirmation answers it.

Sometimes asking the truth about yourself can be difficult and painful, but it releases spiritual energy when you can answer truthfully, even though it may not be the answer you would like to hear. For example, one woman shared with us some of the hard questions she asked herself: "Can I be a truly loving mother since I often feel angry and frustrated with my children? Do I really love them?" In the energy of self-awareness, she was able to

138

answer: "Most of the time I intend to be loving even when I don't *feel* love. I make mistakes, yes, but my choice is to be loving. Therefore, I can affirm that I am a loving parent."

If you seem not to value yourself, begin by honestly asking and answering for yourself the question, "What is the truth about me?" If you have poor self-esteem you probably either don't acknowledge the truth about yourself and therefore misrepresent it, or else you want the truth to be different from what it really is. In the first case, your task is to begin acknowledging the truth. In the second, your task is to create a vision of how you would like yourself to be.

To do either task, kythe with someone you see as having the self-esteem you would like to possess. Since you are present to his or her spirit you will also be able to see yourself at the spirit level. When in kythe you may also observe your partner modeling the behaviors and attitudes you would like to have as your own. Notice how this kything process is a blend of psychological and spiritual activity.

"If I kythe with someone who has high self-esteem," explained a young man, "I would like some of it to flow into me. I could surely use it. But I'd also probably start reflecting on how my kything partner lives his life in light of self-esteem and look for the factors that build his self-esteem. I would want those factors in my life, and I would probably set in motion, consciously or unconsciously, some actions that would bring it about."

This young man is aware that he would have access to his kything partner not only at a spiritual level but also at a behavioral level.

I can remember, reflect, and imagine how I saw him acting at certain times. For example, the next time I find myself in a situation where I perceive someone attacking a statement I have made, instead of getting defensive, retracting or modifying my statement, I can view my kything partner's kind of openness as an alternative way to behave. When his statements are attacked, he doesn't attack back. Instead, he usually points out what is true and helpful about the attacker's comment, points out how it is different from

139

his statement, affirms his own beliefs, and specifies what he doesn't understand.

By kything in this way, the young man can become open to the energy of truth. Since in this new approach he is now essentially asking the attacker "What is the truth here?" he is allowing both himself and the attacker to become conscious of the truth of who they are and to build mutual self-esteem. As he put it, "I seek to know the truth both of who I am and who I am not."

The truth about who we are is usually far more than we would ever imagine. Religions at their best usually call us to be aware of our sublime uniqueness and value in God's eyes.

During a Jewish boy's circumcision an empty chair is placed next to the grandfather's chair near the rabbi. This empty chair is for the prophet Elijah who is believed to be present in spirit to bless the child. In fact, after the foreskin is cut, the child lying on the pillow of circumcision is placed in Elijah's chair (in his lap) to receive the prophet's blessing. The intent of the ceremony is for the child to realize how important he is to God, since Elijah himself comes as God's messenger to bless him and remind him of his high calling as a special child of God and a valuable member of God's people.

We all need the spiritual energy of self-awareness and self-affirmation in order to live up to our high calling as humans. Yet, to become everything we can be also demands the spiritual energy of courage.

Defining Courage

In using kything to develop this third kind of spiritual energy called *courage,* it is important to understand its definition. Courage is *not* the opposite of discouragement or despair. Rather, *courage is the ability to carry on despite discouragement, despair, fear, failure, guilt, or rejection.* More abstractly, courage is a spiritual energy which can operate alongside certain negative psychological energies such as fear, despair, etc. So, even though you feel worthless because you have failed in school, or feel despair because you have been fired from your job, or feel fear of abandonment because you have been rejected by a friend, with courage you still have the energy to go forward with life. As a spiritual energy, courage is a senior force to these negative psychological energies, and can operate effectively even in their presence.

Courage is an energy that enables you to push beyond feelings of insecurity. It enables you to take risks, not just for your own aggrandizement but simply for the human good that can come from what you do. Ultimately, courage refers to the kind of energy that Jesus described when he talked about being willing to lay down your life for your friends.

In 1987, the FBI fired Jack Ryan, a 22-year agency veteran, for refusing to conduct an investigation he believed was morally wrong. Ryan, who was ten months from retirement when he received notice of dismissal, said the inner conflict was between his conscience and an official assignment. "Our policy in Central America is wrong," Ryan explained. "If I help the government stop people who oppose the policy, I'm helping the government carry it out." To act on what he believed to be true and to put his life and security on the line, he needed the spiritual energy of courage. We can be sure that Ryan was scared of what might happen to him and to his job security when he told his supervisors he would be unable to pursue the investigation. But despite his fear he went forward. In a sworn statement to the Bureau he wrote, "For me as an FBI agent to cooperate with such an effort places me directly and firmly in complicity with the activity targeted by the dissent. This is a position I refuse to take."[1]

Are you one of those who would like to be able to make the first move, like Jack Ryan? To speak out for what is true and necessary? To confront misunderstanding? To leave an unhealthy job? To look for work that challenges your highest aspirations? To take action where there is hope of greater good for someone you love?

Would you be willing to pick up and move to a new area of the country for the health of one member of your family? Would you risk losing a relationship in order to be true to yourself? Would you be willing to present

---

[1] Susan Hansen, "FBI Agent Fired in Conflict Between Job and Conscience," *National Catholic Reporter*, October 2, 1987, p. 4.

a story you wrote or a piece of art you made in order to have it criticized? Would you be willing to stand up in front of a crowd to speak about what you truly believe? Would you be willing to change your entire lifestyle if it were necessary to keep your family together? Would you have the courage to support your spouse's career even if it involved your having to change jobs and move? If you would like to be able to do some of these things you may want to build up your courage energy.

Kything for Courage

To kythe for courage, choose someone who possesses the courage you need or want. It may be a friend or acquaintance or a famous person, living or dead. You may of course kythe with more than one courageous person. Using the standard three steps—*Center, Focus, Connect*—kythe with the person you chose.

It helps if you practice kything for courage a number of times before you actually need to exercise your courage in a specific situation. In other words, establish a kything relationship with the courageous person ahead of time, so that when the actual moment comes when you need to display your courage (in front of your boss, in front of an audience, in front of an enemy, etc.) you can re-establish the kythe with your partner easily and quickly. The idea is to have developed a *habit* of connecting with a courageous partner for spiritual strength and mentally practicing having courage.

After the courageous action is done, kythe once again with your partner and express your gratitude.

It is surprising how often we need courage in our everyday lives. For example, if you are about to confront an angry spouse, sit for an examination, go for an important interview, give a speech in public, or do dreamwork on a scary nightmare, you may want to kythe with someone who embodies the courage you want.

A woman was frightened because she felt she had done irreparable harm to her physical system by taking certain diet pills in large doses. "I was really eager to lose weight," she explained, "and I felt that if two pills

142

were good then four or more would work better and faster. I was so scared of what I might have done to myself by taking all those pills that I didn't even want to face a doctor."

She needed courage just to tolerate the truth about her health, so she kythed with a number of people, some of whom were physicians she trusted while others were friends who would want her to be healthy. After kything with them she was able to make the choice to see a doctor and begin treatment to rebalance her physical system.

Kything and Forgiveness

The ability to forgive is really part of the spiritual energy of courage. The need for forgiveness surfaces when a relationship has been harmed, for example, through lying, cheating, betrayal, injury, rejection, failure, etc. An initial state of forgiveness consists in saying, "I forgive you." A second and more courageous stage occurs when you decide about the future of the relationship. In this second stage you may say either "But I never want to see you again" or "Let us go forward together again."

To choose to go forward together again despite betrayal and hurt feelings requires courage. The presumption here is that in choosing to go forward together you have an enduring love for the other person and value the continuation of the relationship; this would normally be the case when forgiveness occurs between family members. However, if the relationship in which the betrayal occurred was not an important relationship, it might be wise to ask yourself if you really want to work at saving it.

It takes courage to recognize and acknowledge the negative feelings caused by the other person and then take a further step, namely, to begin replacing these negative feelings with trust, compassion, caring, and working together. In order to go forward together successfully, it is also important that you accept the other person's limitations of character and establish a loving relationship with that person as he or she is, not with the person you wish he or she were.

Even after you have forgiven the other person, fear and mistrust as psychological feelings may still be present in you and need to be dealt with,

143

but the spiritual energy of courage is a senior force that can carry you beyond your fear and anger in order to help re-create the broken relationship in a healthy, reality-based way.

In forgiving people, you look beyond their offense and see their larger goodness. In loving them for their wholeness and their greater purpose in life, you can view their moment of brokenness as a step on their journey. If you still feel anger toward them, and it is natural that you do, put the anger in a larger perspective. In working through the anger, get in touch with it, own it as your own feeling, let it find appropriate expression (without harming anyone),[2] and finally see it in perspective, that is, as something that has happened in the past and has become a part of the past, no longer to distort and discolor the present and the future.

It should be noted, for example, that if the man you forgave for betraying your confidence has a tendency to gossip, you may need to decide whether you should tell him any more secrets, for he may be unable to keep from betraying you again.

When you forgive someone face-to-face, your live action is usually preceded by an act of inner forgiveness on your part, so that the face-to-face exchange is an outward expression of an inner change that has already taken place. You may use kything as a setting for inner forgiveness, that is, you may work through the forgiveness process at the spiritual level while in kythe with the person. When you reach a state of genuine forgiveness, you can generally feel the shift in your spirit. If afterwards you express your forgiveness verbally, you know your words are authentic.

Forgiveness Without Face-to-Face Contact

With kything, you may also work through forgiveness for a past offense even if the person is no longer physically accessible, either because of death, distance, psychological incompetence, or refusal to meet. Many

---

[2]In the best of circumstances, you and the other person may choose to have a constructive confrontation so that your feelings may be aired and hopefully resolved. In other circumstances, you may express your anger harmlessly through groaning or physical exertion. We recommend a number of ways to release strong feelings in our book *Prayerways*.

children have used kything to bring about an inner reconciliation with their parents who are now dead, or living in other parts of the world or in nursing homes where they are disoriented or senile. Others have kythed forgivingly with spouses or former associates who are bitter and resentful because of separation or misunderstanding, and refuse to communicate in ways that would promote reconciliation.

In kything with such persons, you connect primarily with their spirit, their essence, their wholeness. You are in touch with a dimension of them that is much larger than their failures and hurtful actions.

One woman whose mother had battered her during childhood was finally able to forgive her. The mother suffering from Alzheimer's disease was in a nursing home and no longer even recognized her daughter. When the daughter kythed with her mother she said, "I felt sorrow and compassion for all my mother's wasted life, for her unacknowledged gifts and all her unused potential. I wanted more for her than she was able to want for herself. Now I feel so sad that she deprived herself of so much, that her life was so unlived."

You may also forgive people in kythe who in face-to-face contact would probably not accept forgiveness. Because it is possible to connect with them through kything, forgiveness can at least be effected on the spiritual level, which is a most important level. A woman reported how even years after their divorce her ex-husband was still bitter and refused to communicate with her.

But I was able to kythe with him, and in the kythe I felt him say to me, "I really treated you rather badly and I'm sorry." I heard myself answer, "We were both pretty immature." I heard our dialogue coming from our spirits and felt the truth of it when I was able to look at it from the perspective of the whole person I was and the whole person he was. During the kythe I forgave him and I sensed he forgave me. I'm not sure what it did for him because he still refuses to talk, but it sure made a big difference for peace in my life.

She also felt that if her ex-husband were ever to be open to a discussion she would be much more ready for it after having done a forgiveness kythe with him. She would no longer be on the defensive as she had been.

Self-Forgiveness

One important part of forgiveness is self-forgiveness. The woman in the story above was also in touch with her wish to be forgiven for any of her failings in the relationship. Not only did she want her former partner to forgive her, she also needed to forgive herself.

To deal with self-forgiveness in kything we suggest you kythe with some person you feel is self-forgiving or has the quality of forgiveness and courage. In the kythe ask this person to be present to you as you forgive yourself. Ask the person to be a truth-teller and a truth-reflector for you and to show you how to forgive yourself.

Mike began to realize that he was habitually stingy and thoughtless and that spending as little money as possible was a major value in his life. He felt ashamed to realize that "saving" money had been more important to him than being a good friend and even than being fair in money transactions. He doubted he could ever become the generous and thoughtful person he wanted to be, a person like Ted who was generous toward himself as well as toward others. So Mike kythed with Ted and was able to forgive himself for being stingy and thoughtless, as he knew Ted would do. Now, as he is trying to shift his value system and place generosity near the top, he often kythes with Ted not only to forgive himself for lapses into stinginess but also to learn how to be more thoughtful and generous.

15. Kything and Compassion

Compassion

Whenever the rabbi of Sasov saw anyone's suffering either of spirit or of body, he shared it so earnestly that the other's suffering became his own. Once somebody expressed amusement at this capacity to share in another's troubles. "What do you mean 'share'?" said the rabbi. "It is my own sorrow. How can I help but suffer it?"[1]

As a spiritual energy, fourth on the list, *compassion* is the ability to be unconditionally loving. Most of us put conditions and expectations on people we love, and we often threaten to withhold our love until others fulfill certain conditions. To get a sense of how people impose conditions on their expression of love, simply ask yourself to list the qualities you look for and often require in your friends, your spouse, your children, your business associates. As you compile your list—kind, gentle, thoughtful, clean, neat, sympathetic, honest, open, dependable, generous, attractive, etc.—realize that each item is a condition or an expectation placed on the relationship. In effect we say, "I won't love you if you behave badly," "I won't love you when you are depressed or angry," "I won't love you till you get a better job," "I won't love you unless you agree with me."

When love is unconditional, there are no such lists.

---

[1]Martin Buber, *Tales of Hasidism—Late Masters.* New York: Schocken Books, 1948, p. 86.

In this sense, compassion is a prerequisite to deep kything, for the conditions and expectations we place on others or ourselves often keep us or distract us from the depth of communion of which we are capable.

Harper Lee's novel *To Kill a Mockingbird* offers a simple description of compassion:

> "First of all," he said, "if you can learn a simple trick, Scout, you'll get along a lot better with all kinds of folks. You never really understand a person until you consider things from his point of view...."
>
> "Sir?"
>
> "...until you climb into his skin and walk around in it."

Compassion is the ability to walk in another's shoes, to feel what he or she is feeling and in general to experience the world the way he or she experiences it. When you kythe, like the rabbi of Sasov you are fully open to another's spirit and experience.

Compassion Versus Identification

Compassion is different from *identification,* as psychologists normally use the term.[2]

When you "identify" with someone, according to most psychologists, you use an experience of another person in order to release unconscious feelings you have toward a similar issue or experience in your own life. For example, a death of someone's best friend reminds me of the death of someone close to me. While I may genuinely feel sorry for the person whose friend has died, *in identification most of my emotion has to do with my own grief and loss,* of which I am unconscious. I identify (or equate my-

---

[2]Alfred Adler is a striking exception. In his psychology he defines "identification" in much the same way we describe "compassion." So for Adler and for most people in ordinary conversation, "to identify with" and "to have compassion for" are synonymous. In this book we view them as two different processes.

self) with the other person in order to work on my own grief. In identification, I don't really relate to the other person as a person but rather as a vehicle to release my own emotions.

On the other hand, compassion is precisely a relational experience. During it, like the rabbi of Sasov, you are in touch with the other person and their current unique situation without losing your own identity, wisdom, and understanding. You stay present to the other person and their problem without getting absorbed in your own issues.

When you kythe with compassion you use your affective imagination to experience what it would feel like if you were the other person, with his or her personality and circumstances, experiencing this unique moment of grief. In other words, "you climb into his skin and walk around in it." Or, as Walt Whitman put it in *Leaves of Grass:*

> Agonies are one of my changes of garments.
> I do not ask the wounded person how he feels,
> I myself become the wounded person.

It is possible to move from identification to compassion if you are conscious of it. A counselor at a women's hospital describes how she went from identifying with a client to building a relationship of compassion with her.

> The young mother was a poor black woman whose husband had left her when she was pregnant, and I was facilitating her in working through blocked grief for her premature child who was dying. I identified with her situation when I recalled how my husband had left me when I was pregnant. I began to cry. I told her that she wasn't making me cry, but that her story had put me in touch with my own grief. (Incidentally, my tears allowed her to get in touch with her own grief.)
>
> It was clear to me that I was identifying, because our situations were similar but not identical. She was poor, black, and uneducated, while I was white, middle-class, and well-educated.

149

One thing she had that I didn't have was a deeply caring family of origin. My family were not a loving bunch.

Once I was able to recognize and move beyond my own identification, I was able to shift to a place of empathy and compassion, and be with her where she truly was, with her own unique strengths, weaknesses, and resources. That's when I was able to kythe with her and to feel my caring and loving for the unique person she was. I could then see her as a real person and not as some shadow of myself with which I identified. In this shift a special bonding occurred between us. I learned what she needed from me and how to give it. She learned about the support she needed and could get from me and others, and how to receive it. She learned something about who she was, I learned something about who I was, and we both learned something about each other and our relationship.

In compassion-kything you have a direct knowing of another's grief (or joy or love or anything else). You know it because, like Walt Whitman, you become present to the other in his or her totality. You can't really know a person's unique grief (or joy or anything else) until you become one with the person who is having the feelings. This oneness is not just an intellectual process but involves the knowing of another's spirit through your spirit. In kything you know how something feels to other persons and what it means to *them* because you can be with them and *in* them.

A child psychologist working with a boy who was learning-disabled describes how she was able to empathize with him and know *his* joy.

Seven-year-old Albert was treated as a retarded and undesirable child by his classmates and teachers, and because of his bizarre behavior was removed from school. Albert and I worked together for a whole year until he was ready to step back into the classroom. At our final therapy session, I held out to him the drum we had been using all year to learn sounds and rhythms for reading-readiness, and I told him that he could keep it. I told him that

150

I wanted him to have this drum that he had enjoyed so much; it was his now. He smiled at me as he accepted the gift.

You have to know something about Albert's blackness, poverty, deprivation, and his being avoided and undervalued in order to be with him in his joy—that our work together had been successful and he had been accepted in a regular school and would be seen as a regular child! In a way this was his graduation into being like other children. Because I knew his spirit and we had been spiritually connected for months through kything, I could rejoice in the richness and uniqueness of who he was and what he had accomplished. I could rejoice *in* him.

Kything and the Unborn

A very special kind of kything can happen with the unborn. We heard of an expectant father who used to come home from work each evening and while his pregnant wife lay on the couch resting he would put his face near the baby and speak to it. He wanted the baby to hear his voice and to know that he loved it. He told the baby about the world awaiting it. He was establishing a bond of love and joy with the child in the womb.

When we described kything to him, he thanked us for the new word and announced that this is what he had been doing all along. He had learned to do it spontaneously.

It is not necessary to be a baby's parents to be able to kythe with a new human life even before it is born.

16. Kything, Commitment, Discernment, and Cosmic Consciousness

Kything and Commitment

The fifth kind of spiritual energy, *commitment,* is associated with the powers of your will. Roberto Assagioli in his book *The Act of Will* accords to the will a pre-eminent position in psychology and regards it as "the central element and direct expression of the 'I,' or self."[1] This central place may not be so clear when psychologists and philosophers attempt to assess the role of the will on purely theoretical lines, says Assagioli, but it becomes evident as soon as we observe the direct, existential experience of willing. In simple language, we are what we choose, we are free to make choices, and these choices shape our life and our destiny.

We have chosen to characterize the spiritual energy related to the will as *commitment,* but it also includes decisiveness, determination, perseverance, the ability to make decisions and to carry them out.

How many times have you made a decision or a resolution with the best of intentions only to discover a few days later that you have slipped back into your old patterns? This spiritual energy gives you the ability to make a decision and to stick to it, to bring about the result you truly want. It is the quality of fidelity to your word and faithfulness to a relationship or to yourself.

When you are about to make a new resolution in a difficult matter,

---

[1] Roberto Assagioli, M.D., *The Act of Will.* New York: Viking, 1973, p. 245.

kythe with persons whom you know that have this energy. Let them be a part of your decision-making and a part of carrying it out. Later, when you are tempted to let your resolve slip, treat this as a strategically important moment and kythe with such persons for the energy to stay committed to the promise you made.

Kything and Discernment

There are myriad places where we need the sixth kind of spiritual energy characterized as *wisdom and discernment*. We need it for making good choices; for understanding the meaning of an event, a person, or the way God is working in our life; for clarifying who I am and who I am not; for seeing opportunities and recognizing true potential; for recognizing the difference between risk-taking and foolhardiness, between surrender and passivity, between impulse and intuition; for knowing when to push and when to wait; for being able to detect and name an inner movement of the spirit; for knowing the truth when I come upon it; for giving appropriate names to persons, things, feelings and events; for noticing the "just perceptible difference"; for knowing when to trust someone and when not; for knowing when to place a responsibility on someone (e.g., knowing when a child is old enough to accept certain responsibilities); for recognizing the difference between loving a child and over-indulgence, between forgiveness and an inability to set limits, between teaching and moralizing.

Kythe with those who have wisdom and discernment, and ask for the energy to accept and express these qualities in your life. When you kythe, it may be helpful to imagine you and your kything partner in a wisdom-moment. Picture wisdom energy flowing between you.

In selecting kything partners for wisdom and discernment, don't overlook children. Youngsters often present us with wisdom beyond their years—as if their spirits or souls were very old and wise. Furthermore, they are often able to see with eyes that are as yet unclouded by the prevailing culture.

A family who had lived in a beautiful home in the country for ten years were very sad at having to move to the city, even though it meant an important promotion for the father. Amid all their sadness and anger at having to uproot themselves from this beautiful spot, the twelve-year-old daughter in a moment of wisdom said, "Let's remember how lucky we are to have lived in this place for ten whole years. We have been very happy here and have lots of lovely memories to treasure. Now it's somebody else's turn."

Make a list of the people you think of as wise and discerning (not merely intelligent). Select any of these people for kything partners whenever you need the gifts of wisdom and discernment.

Wisdom and discernment may also be very helpful in spiritual direction.

Kything and Spiritual Direction

Many of the ideas we have shared about kything and the therapist also apply to the spiritual director. Although kything is available to the client alone or to the spiritual director alone, it can also profitably be used by the client and spiritual director together.

We envision the spiritual director teaching kything to clients who are unfamiliar with the process, teaching it as a basic skill for spiritual growth and as a way for client and director to build a relationship of trust at the level of spirit. (We presume that both client and director are comfortable with the idea of kything. Please don't encourage kything with each other if either of you is not comfortable with it.)

If both of you have made a commitment to work together and that commitment is open to mutual spiritual presence, you may agree to kythe with each other at the beginning of each session and to be open to kything at other times.

Kything and Cosmic Consciousness

The seventh and final kind of spiritual energy we want to talk about in this chapter is hard to describe. People have called *cosmic consciousness* by different names such as the unitive experience, the oceanic experience, divine perspective, the big picture. The point is that this spiritual energy gives you the capacity to look at your life and the world from a perspective that is much more cosmic in scope than your ego. Even Sigmund Freud recognized this capacity, though he attributed it only to infants, claiming that we lost it as we grew up in a civilized world.

> Originally the ego includes everything; later it detaches from itself the external world. The ego-feeling we are aware of now is thus only a shrunken vestige of a far more extensive feeling—*a feeling which embraced the universe* and expressed an inseparable connection of the ego with the external world.[2]

Cosmic consciousness involves seeing your life not merely from the present moment but from a transcendent moment. When those with whom you kythe invite you to look at your life from the perspective of eternity, the way God looks at it, they are calling forth this spiritual energy in you. From this perspective, as the poet William Wordsworth described it, you see "Intimations of Immortality."

This seventh kind of spiritual energy allows you to see the sweep of evolution, to see the planet as one organism, to feel an integral part of a magnificent, living totality.

What is special about kything is that it makes the physical, material world very available to you. The rocks, rivers, mountains, trees, and the air itself become a part of your spiritual process and not separate from your spirit. Kything helps you to understand the unity and necessity of matter and spirit.

When you stand on a windswept beach and feel a unity with nature, you are experiencing this unitive energy. When you hold a newborn baby close to your body and feel the shared aliveness with it and with everything else, you are experiencing this universal energy. When you read books written hundreds of years ago and time collapses so that you can sense the presence of the ancient authors and their wisdom here and now, you are experiencing this transcendent energy.

---

[2]Sigmund Freud, *Civilization and Its Discontents.* London: Hogarth Press, 1949, p. 13. Italics added.

One of the most outstanding inventors and electronic geniuses of this century was Nikola Tesla, a Croatian originally from Yugoslavia, who learned how to become spiritually present to people and places from within this cosmic consciousness. He attributes much of his creativity to his spiritual travels. He describes his growing ability:

> I saw new scenes. These were at first blurred and indistinct and would flit away when I tried to concentrate my attention on them. They gained strength and distinctness and finally assumed the concreteness of real things. I soon discovered that my best comfort was attained if I simply went on in my vision further and further, getting new impressions all the time, and so I began to travel; of course, in my mind. Every night, and sometimes during the day, when alone, I would start on my journeys, see new places, cities and countries, live there, meet people and make friendships and acquaintances and, however unbelievable, it is a fact that they were just as dear to me as those in actual life, and not a bit less intense in their manifestations.[3]

To most people, such inner travels seem bizarre, reserved only to crazy inventors and religious mystics. How sad that spiritual capacities available to everyone are so seldom used. A wise old psychiatrist once said that most people in therapy were there because they were spending so much of their energy *avoiding* living up to their highest potential. How sad that people are unwilling to be different, to stand out from the crowd, in order to live up to their highest. Why do so many want to be lost in the crowd? Author David Riesman in his book *The Lonely Crowd* quoted a twelve-year-old girl who summed up what he thought was the reason: "I would like to be able to fly if everyone else did," she said, "but otherwise it would be kind of conspicuous."

According to Alan Watts, without this seventh kind of spiritual energy

---

[3]Christopher Bird and Oliver Nichelson, "Great Scientist, Forgotten Genius: Nikola Tesla," in *New Age Magazine,* February 1977, p. 38.

flowing in your life, living feels restricted, dry, lonely. In his book *Nature, Man and Woman,* he writes:

> Ecstasy, or transcending oneself, is the natural accompaniment of a full relationship in which we experience the "inner identity" between ourselves and the world. But when that relationship is hidden and the individual feels himself to be a restricted island of consciousness, his emotional experience is largely one of restriction, and it is as arid as the abstract *persona* which he believes himself to be.[4]

Despite the fact, as Freud implies, that most of us have lost touch with this capacity to experience the oneness of all creation, there are many who still feel it. For example, it is probably the spiritual energy felt by those who have dedicated themselves to the ecology movement, to missionary work, to world peace, to the fellowship of all humans, to the exploration of space, to programs like Amnesty International, Save the Whales, the Peace Corps. All of these endeavors share a dimension that calls people to see the larger world beyond their own selves and families. They see all human beings—in fact, all things animate and inanimate—as brothers and sisters meant to live together in creativity and peace.

As a hasidic master once wrote about experiencing this spiritual energy of union while kything with nature:

> When you walk across the fields with your mind pure and holy, then from all the stones, and all growing things, and all animals, the sparks of their soul come out and cling to you, and then they are purified and become a holy fire in you.[5]

---

[4]Alan W. Watts, *Nature, Man and Woman.* New York: Mentor, 1938, p. 132.

[5]Martin Buber, *Tales of Hasidism—Later Masters.* New York: Schocken Books, 1948, p. 86.

Individual and Cosmos

On the one hand, you are a uniquely individual human being. On the other hand, as the physicists researching the "biodance" see it, you are part of the total cosmos. You are interrelated with all and everything. You are inextricably woven into the total universe.

When kything, it is this second perspective, the unity of all things, that is seen as most important. The focus is on the network of relationships rather than on individual uniqueness. The ordinary way of perceiving reality begins with each thing, entity or event seen as something separate and unique. In kything, this ordinary perception of reality is reversed. It begins with the new realization that I can be present to all things and all things can be present to me, and I can live in all things and all can live in me. We are in total communion. In short, with whatever is, I can fuse without confusion.

In ordinary consciousness, time flows continually and relentlessly forward; it can't be stopped, slowed down, speeded up or reversed. In kything consciousness, all things *are;* they do not happen in succession. Because kything occurs in the domain of spirit, past, present, and future are equally in existence and available to my spirit.

17. Kything with Animals and Nature

Kything with Animals

I have always loved animals. When I was young, I used to talk to them a lot. Well, not really talk. I felt a sense of touching their minds. Sometimes I would use words to do this, but the words were mainly for my own sake. The animals didn't need to hear me talk. Actually, I really didn't even talk very much. Usually I would sit or stand quietly and sort of think or send "peace" to an animal. When I did this, the animals would often turn and look at me as if someone had "touched" them. But, after a while, they got to know my "touch" and some of them would come up to me—rabbits, squirrels, frogs, deer. It didn't seem to matter if they were wild or tame, they'd come anyway. When they came, I would stay quietly where I was or, if I moved, it was gently and slowly, always holding them in my loving feelings. I used my mind and my heart to do this. I used to practice sending love and peace to almost all animals but especially to my pets and my friends' pets. I didn't think it was so special then. I just liked to do it. I guess I thought everyone did it or could do it.

The young woman who told us this story was, in her own way, kything with these animals. She was spiritually connecting with them, and they felt it. As soon as we explained about kything, she said she thought it was a funny name, but agreed it described what she had been doing better than the phrase "talking to the animals" did.

Our discussion of kything reminded her of another story about communicating with a mouse. She smiled as she recounted the story.

> I remember a mouse we had in our house some years ago. I had seen it a number of times and sort of smiled at it when I saw it. I even sent it peace and love as I used to do with the animals on the farm. I thought that mouse was cute, and I guess I loved it the way I tend to do with most animals. However, we had a part-time housekeeper who didn't like mice at all. Shaking her broom, she muttered something to me about seeing a mouse and planning to get rid of it. I guess I thought about the poor creature and realized I didn't want it to get hurt, because the next day when I was in the kitchen alone, the mouse came out and sat up on its haunches on the floor in front of me, as if to say, "We need to talk about this situation I'm in." I put out my loving presence to it, the way you said about kything, and explained to the mouse that things were too dangerous around here, with the housekeeper out to kill it, and that it would have to find another place to live for its own good. That little mouse, sitting there just a few feet from my foot, seemed to be listening intently, because when I was finished talking it turned around and went slowly into a hole near a radiator pipe. I never saw it again. Neither did the housekeeper.

She told us that, with animals, all you have to do is project your loving feelings or loving presence toward them. When you do, they will often come closer. Usually they will let you come closer. And sometimes they will even let you get close enough to touch them. "I think every child who truly loves animals automatically sends out a loving presence," she explained, "and when this happens animals aren't afraid and are approachable. But if you're not truly loving or are full of fears, the animals will know it, probably be afraid, and keep their distance."

J. Allen Boone in his two books, *Kinship with All Life* and *The Language of Silence,* describes dozens of heartwarming experiences like these that reveal a wonderful communion between human beings and animals.

Boone was asked to tutor and take charge of Strongheart, the dog who starred in such Hollywood movies as *The Silent Call, Brawn of the North, The Love Master,* and Jack London's *White Fang.* He tells how Strongheart apparently mind-read his thoughts and feelings. Here is one story.

> I did not have to be within range of Strongheart's physical observation for him correctly to read my thinking and know all about my plans. He could do it across distances as easily as though he were sitting at my side. For instance, once or twice each week I would have luncheon at a Los Angeles club that was over a dozen miles away from where Strongheart and I lived. Whenever I did this a friend would stay at the house and keep an eye on the dog. There was never any set time for my returning, but at the precise moment when I decided to leave the club and come home Strongheart would always quit whatever he happened to be doing, take himself to his favorite spot for observation, and patiently wait there for me to turn the bend in the road and head up the hill.[1]

Allen Boone admired the American Indians and their ability to get along with animals. He believed that the Indians exuded a mental and spiritual atmosphere that was like an invisible handshake of good will toward other creatures. He learned to proffer this invisible handshake to animals just as the Indians did.

Once during a motion picture location trip into the African jungles with Douglas Fairbanks, Allen refused to carry weapons. He trusted that all the jungle creatures he met, despite their bad reputations, would be friendly if his thoughts about them were friendly. He observed that most of the natives didn't carry weapons either. He explained: "The natives have a mental rapport with the animals. With those who know it and practice it, there is

---

[1] J. Allen Boone, *Kinship with All Life.* New York: Harper & Row, 1954, p. 41.

an interrelating oneness between the human and the creature. I have to be right myself mentally to experience it."[2]

One element in this right attitude is to have a sense of equality when dealing with animals. It is too easy for us humans, Boone felt, to see ourselves as incomparably higher up in the scale of life and animals far below us as lesser creatures, and to treat them as such. The invisible bridge connecting us with the animals, spirit-to-spirit, needs to be perfectly horizontal. The relationship should be equal and reciprocal. When Allen Boone set up this horizontal bridge and invited two-way thought traffic, "the easier it became for that monkey [or other animal] and me to share ourselves in the universal harmony and rhythm of 'We-Us-and-Our.' "[3]

Steps To Kythe with Animals

If you wish to kythe with an animal, it may be easiest to begin with your pet or an animal who knows you.

Use the standard three steps in kything: First, take a deep breath or two to get centered in yourself. Second, hold an image of the pet in your imagination, and do it lovingly. Perhaps you can breathe out love through your heart toward it, and picture it in your imagination as surrounded with a glowing light of love. Third, picture you and the pet connected (perhaps both you and it surrounded by the same circle of light) and choose the connection.

You may of course kythe while you are physically holding the pet, but there is no need for physical touch or presence. In order to kythe with an animal there is no need to physically look at it or hold it, but of course you can, and many people prefer this to intensify the kything experience. However, it is enough to picture the kything connection in your imagination. As Allen Boone observed, a beloved pet like Strongheart is probably already in continuous touch with your mind and spirit.

As one man who feels spiritually connected to his dog told us, "Often

[2]. J. Allen Boone, *The Language of Silence.* New York: Harper & Row, 1970, p. x.
[3] *Ibid.,* p. 11.

when Brandy is sitting in my lap and I think to myself, 'I wonder if it's time to put him out for a while,' he jumps off my lap and goes to the kitchen door to be let out."

People sometimes ask if they can do a healing kythe with an animal. The answer is yes. You can kythe with an animal both to help heal the animal and to help heal yourself.

We invite you to use your own unique creativity in exploring the world of kything with animals.

Kything With Flowers, Plants, and Trees

As we have mentioned, you may kythe with anything that has a spirit, and all living things have a spiritual dimension.

It is common knowledge that people "talk" to plants, and that plants are sensitive to human emotions and to the rhythms and vibrations of music. Plants seem to be able to sense human feelings and intentions, even if they can't understand conceptual language. For an introduction to the ways that plants are spiritually connected to each other and to humans, see a wonderful book by Peter Tompkins and Christopher Bird called *The Secret Life of Plants.*[4]

We find that people kythe with trees, plants, flowers, and other parts of nature mostly for their own healing, wholeness, and enjoyment. Often the energies you may need may be found in a flower, a plant or a tree. Connecting yourself with the earth's energies is a way of grounding yourself and of affirming the total bondedness of all creation.

Here kything becomes a gesture of rooting; using it you connect yourself by means of your spiritual oneness to the roots of nature, thus breaking through the fundamental loneliness and apartness people often feel.

One young man during recuperation from burnout used to kythe with a large oak tree in a nearby park. Each day he would sit near the tree and connect with it spirit-to-spirit. He became aware of how it lifted its branches

---

[4]Peter Tompkins and Christopher Bird, *The Secret Life of Plants.* New York: Harper & Row, 1973.

toward heaven, opening its leaves to all the available energy of the sun, the air, and the rain while its roots, hidden from view, reached deep into the earth to tap the energies available to it there. The young man began to learn of his own need for deep connection to the earth—in caring for his body which he had neglected—as well as an outward reach to sources of emotional nourishment available to him from his friends and family. The tree, he felt, gave him a sense of rootedness and also a desire to aspire toward wholeness.

Plants, flowers, and trees have certain energies and qualities that we can use for our healing and wholeness. Trees, for example, have a marvelous patience, beauty, and gracefulness. They are able to sway with strong forces, to find nourishment deep within themselves and the earth, to deal with hurt or abuse, to heal themselves even after amputation, to renew themselves, and to give birth to others of their own kind.

To kythe with a plant or tree, choose a favorite or one that attracts you, then think of its qualities and energies that you need and would like to have and share.

Nature offers many new dimensions of relating through spiritual communion. It helps us recognize our oneness and indebtedness to all creation.

As the artist Gordon Onslow Ford said, "As separate beings, we are not self-sufficient. We are able to live because we are sustained by the environment. Thus it is only natural that we should be grateful to all that supports our life: the stars, the stones, the vegetation, the animals, human beings and their works. In giving thanks, we become open to dimensions beyond the purely personal."[5]

If we are all part of the organic unity that makes up the entire cosmos, there is nothing to bar information or energy being exchanged between us. In this light, St. Paul wrote to the people of Ephesus about the importance of truth: "Let everyone speak the truth to his neighbor, for we are members of one another."[6] Nothing can come between me and the rest of the cosmos.

---

[5]The Frontispiece, *Noetic Sciences Review*, Autumn 1987.
[6]*Paul's Letter to the Ephesians* 4:25.

As one of our students put it:

The first time I kythed with a flower, I realized I could kythe with all creation. And a startling possibility has entered my mind: Through kything loneliness is no more. I realized another thing too. The energy in the suffering of loneliness is the spirit pushing for relationship.

To think of the possibilities that exist if everyone were to consciously practice kything with all elements of creation is almost beyond belief. What a support system! What a way of awakening all the love and spiritual energy that is available in our very own world!

As the poet William Blake once wrote:

Arise and drink your bliss;
For everything that lives is holy.

Kything
and the
Sacred

18. Kything and Jesus Christ

Kything: Natural and Sacred

All along we have said that kything is a natural human act. That is, it takes no more supernatural grace to make it happen than it takes to make you talk, move your hands or recall a memory. People are by nature spiritual, so it is just as natural to exercise one's spiritual capacities as it is to exercise one's physical and mental faculties.

Kything may also be treated as a sacred or religious act. That is, it can be brought into the realm of the sacred and used in religious ritual, worship, and prayer. Since the religious tradition with which we are most familiar is the Christian tradition, specifically the Roman Catholic heritage, we have been able to make many applications of the practice of kything to Christian life in its theology and practice. Although we have alluded to some of these sacred applications of kything earlier in the book, we want to develop its theological and biblical connections more fully here.

What makes any activity (including kything) sacred are: (1) the context of the action and (2) one's intention and choice in doing it. Thus, a kiss which is a natural human gesture becomes a sacred act during the Kiss of Peace in eucharistic worship.[1] By context and intention the kiss is trans-

---

[1] The "holy kiss" was quite common in the early Christian community. In almost every letter from Paul in the New Testament occurs the request: "Salute one another with a holy kiss" (Rom 16:16; 1 Cor 16:20; 2 Cor 13:12; 1 Thes 5:26). Peter also encouraged this practice (see 1 Pet 5:14). The holy kiss was evidently more than a simple greeting of friends. Among the believers it was seen as a touching of souls and as an exchange of the Holy Spirit's breath which dwelt in each of them.

169

formed from a merely natural act into a sacred ritual. For worshipers a sacred transformation occurs with the sacramental bread and wine used in the Christian liturgy. The same can be true for kything. By context and intention, it may be transformed into a sacred action.

Jesus and Kything

It is our belief that Jesus was not only familiar with what we call kything, but that it was an important part of his vision of the kingdom of God.

During Jesus' final discourse at the Passover supper he makes striking use of the preposition "in." We feel that he used this preposition to describe a spirit-to-spirit or soul-to-soul presence that was to characterize relationships in the kingdom of God. For example, he used "in" to characterize his relationship with God whom he named *Abba,* which means Father: "Do you believe that I am *in* the Father and the Father is *in* me? The words I speak are not spoken of myself; it is the Father who lives *in* me accomplishing his works" (Jn 14:10).

Not only are the Father and Jesus indwelling in each other and working through each other, but so are the disciples dwelling in them. According to Jesus' vision, "On that day you will know that I am *in* my Father, and you *in* me and I *in* you" (Jn 14:20).

Nor does Jesus exclude from the indwelling anyone who loves him and believes in him. "Any who love me will be true to my word, and my Father will love them; we will come to them and make our dwelling place *in* them" (Jn 14:23). John's First Epistle is also filled with assertions of this mutual indwelling: "No one has ever seen God; but as long as we love one another God will live *in* us and his love will be complete in us. We can know that we are living *in* him and he is living *in* us because he lets us share his Spirit" (1 Jn 4:12–13).[2]

Moreover, Jesus asserts that all future believers will participate in this

---

[2]See also 1 Jn 1:3, 6, 7; 2:5, 6, 14, 24, 28; 3:6, 17, 24; 4:12–16; 5:10, 12, 20.

mutual indwelling. "I pray also for those, Father, who will believe in me through their word, that all of them may be one in the same way as you, Father, are *in* me and I *in* you. I pray that they may be one *in* us" (Jn 17:20).

Relating to Others in Christ

Wouldn't it be natural for all those unconditionally loving persons throughout the centuries who related spirit-to-spirit to Jesus to want to re-late spirit-to-spirit with each other? It is hard to imagine that every Christian wants merely to be "alone with Christ alone." After all, part of the joy of being *in* Christ is to share loving and caring with the many others who are also *in* Christ.

This mutual indwelling among the believers was a primary experience in the early Christian community. As John described it, "What we have seen and heard we are telling you, *so that you too may be in union with us,* as we are in union with the Father and with his Son Jesus Christ" (1 Jn 1:3).

In Jesus' mind there seemed to be no question about the nature of this indwelling union. He experienced it as a mutually and usually simultaneous being in and living in each other. No matter whether you follow the Greek or Hebrew sources of the New Testament, Jesus was clearly using the prep-osition "in." People commonly know what it means to be *with* someone, *beside* someone, *above* someone, or *beneath* someone. But *in* someone? Obviously Jesus is referring to something other than physical presence.

Except for references in the literature of Christian friendship,[3] few the-ologians have explored what it means experientially to be *in* someone and to dwell *in* someone. There is, of course, much literature among the spir-itual writers dealing with the practice of the presence of God, but little or no treatment of the practice of spiritual presence among believers or of their mutual indwelling in spirit.[4] With one exception.

---

[3]See Chapter 1, "Spiritual Presence Among Friends," for a few examples.

[4]Many have asserted the theological doctrine that all of the faithful live in Christ, but few if any have offered practical ways to facilitate the relationships among believers in Christ.

Co-Inherence

In his book *The Descent of the Dove: A Short History of the Holy Spirit in the Church,* Charles Williams recognized the permanent mutual indwelling of God in us, us in God, and *us in each other* (in Christ). Williams called this mutual indwelling "co-inherence," and saw it as the central reality of Christian life.

Theologically, indwelling is an attempt to name and describe the special permanent and habitual personal presence of God in the soul of a person, a presence different from God's universal omnipresence by virtue of creation. Divine indwelling as Jesus described it is not merely an imprint or image of God upon the soul, but the very presence of God: God takes up home in the person's soul. This spiritual and sacred presence enables the person to know and love God directly and immediately.

Williams asked the next logical question. Is there also a spiritual and sacred way for believers to know and love each other directly, spirit-to-spirit? The tradition of spirituality considers indwelling (or co-inherence) merely as the mutual indwelling of God in us and us in God; it does not really treat the issue of co-inherence of us in each other. Williams was perhaps the first to claim that there must have been a technique to practice this co-inherence—a technique that was perhaps known only to a few. As organizations tended to dominate the communities of believers, he wrote, "the practice of the co-inherence seemed driven back more and more secretly into the hearts of the saints, who are few in any age."[5]

Whatever technique this was or whoever were the few who knew it, Williams did not mention it or them. Neither did he claim that he knew how to practice this mutual indwelling. We suspect that the "lost" technique was something like kything, or perhaps the "holy kiss."

Williams reminded us that, throughout the centuries, men and women in the Church have built religious orders and communities dedicated to

---

[5]Charles Williams, *The Descent of the Dove.* Written in 1939 and reprinted in 1979 by Eerdmans Pub. Co., Grand Rapids, Mich., p. 117.

poverty, obedience, preaching, fasting, education, care of the sick, and so on, but none dedicated to the practice of co-inherence. In his book he called for the creation of a Community of the Co-inherence whose mission would be to foster the awareness and conscious practice of mutual indwelling. "The technique needs much discovery," he wrote; "the Order would have no easy labor. But, more than can be imagined, it might find that in this present world its labor was never more needed, its concentration never more important, its profits never perhaps more great."[6]

Kything is a beginning of the "discovery" Williams called for, the development of a technique not only to make this indwelling of God in persons and persons in God more conscious, but also and perhaps more importantly for our day, to facilitate the exchanges of love in mutual indwelling that Christians are called upon to make with each other *in* Christ. "I give you a new commandment: Love one another. Just as I have loved you, you also must love one another. By this love you have for one another everyone will know that you are my disciples" (Jn 13:34). Jesus loved his disciples by co-inherence; if they are to love each other in the same way, it will be by their mutual co-inherence. The world will recognize the presence of Christ by his followers' ability to be present to each other, spirit-to-spirit. As Williams put it, "Within that sublime co-inherence all our lesser co-inherences inhere."[7]

---

[6]*Ibid.,* p. 236.

[7]*Ibid.,* p. 235. Earlier in this book we used the expression "coinherence kythe" to describe a special kind of kything union; our use of the term is different from Williams' generic usage. If you read his book you will see that he uses "co-inherence" to describe a variety of human and sacramental experiences that produce mutual influence or inner effects but not necessarily mutual spiritual presence: for example, the child in the womb for nine months "literally co-inheres in its mother" (p. 234); the child about to be born "already co-inheres in an ancestral and contemporary guilt" [i.e., original sin] (p. 234); in baptism the infant passes into the Church through co-inherence—"from the most material co-inherence it is received into the supernatural" (p. 235); and in the body of Jesus is "the co-inherence of matter and deity" (p. 119). Thus, insofar as he uses the term co-inherence to describe mutual spiritual indwelling, it agrees with our use of the term kything, which is the only meaning we ascribe to the term.

Christian Kything

For believers, the primary indwelling takes place with Jesus Christ: they dwell in Christ and Christ dwells in them. To consciously kythe with Christ, use the basic formula presented in Chapter 2:

(1) When you have centered, say aloud or to yourself, **"I am present to myself."**

(2) When you have formed an image of Christ and hold him in a loving gaze, say to him in spirit, **"I am present to your spirit."**

(3) When you have established a connection through imagery with Christ, choose to make the union explicitly conscious by saying, **"You and I are one"** or **"We are present spirit-to-spirit"** or **"I live in you and you live in me."** Find some expression, perhaps with a biblical flavor, that feels right to you in expressing this union.

If you need suggestions for centering or focusing, review Chapter 2 which discusses the three basic steps of the kything process in detail.

For those who want to kythe with other persons **in** Christ, here is a simple adaptation of the three-step process of kything:

(1) When you have gotten centered and are present to yourself, say aloud or to yourself, **"I am alive in Christ."** You may, for example, picture yourself surrounded by a white light symbolizing Christ's Spirit.

(2) When you are focused lovingly on the other person with whom you want to kythe, holding them in an image, say to him or her in spirit, **"You are alive in Christ."** Here you may picture the other person surrounded by the white light of Christ's Spirit.

(3) When you establish an image that connects you with the other person, perhaps by picturing both of you together surrounded by the Christ-light, choose the union by saying to the other in spirit, **"Together we are one in Christ."**

This sacred kything formula is appropriate for all creatures who have a spiritual dimension; that includes persons alive on earth or in the communion of saints, any of the angelic beings, and all other living things that are joined to us in creation and form a part of the universal Christ.

We cannot stress enough the importance of the first step in kything: centering. This is an essential of the kything process. As Thomas E. Clarke has expressed it, your center is the place of meeting of the human spirit and the divine Spirit, where in fact you can meet "the whole of reality, divine and human, persons and things, time and space, nature and history."[8] When centering is carried out properly and entered into deeply, it often makes the difference between a kythe that is felt and truly experienced, and one that is "taken on faith."

A Healing Kythe in Christ

For those in the Christian ministry of healing, kything with the healee *in* Christ is a natural first step to any other healing prayers.

Here is a simple adaptation of the three-step process for kything in Christ:

1. When you are centered, speak aloud or to yourself some affirmation of health, such as, **"I am alive and whole in Christ,"** or **"I am healthy and whole in Christ,"** or **"I am healed and made whole in Christ."** You may, for example, picture yourself surrounded by Christ's healing light or touched by his healing hand or penetrated by his healing gaze.
2. When you are focused lovingly on the healee, holding the healee in an image, for example, surrounded by Christ's healing light, etc., say to the healee in spirit, **"You are alive and whole in Christ,"** or **"You are healthy and whole in Christ,"** or **"You are healed and made whole in Christ."**

---

[8]Thomas E. Clarke, S.J., "Finding Grace at the Center," in the book of the same name edited by Thomas Keating, O.C.S.O., M. Basil Pennington, O.C.S.O., and Thomas E. Clarke, S.J. Still River, MA: St. Bede Publications, 1978, p. 50.

3. When you establish an image of you and the healee physically connected, perhaps by picturing both of you surrounded by Christ's healing light, choose the union by saying to the healee in spirit, **"Together we are one and whole in Christ,"** or **"Together we are healthy and whole in Christ,"** or **"Together we are healed and made whole in Christ."**

Once again, it is important to remember that the particular affirmations you use simply help you consciously mark the three steps of the healing kythe. They are not magical formulas. You may create your own affirmations or use none at all, though most people find the three affirmations useful and helpful.

Theologically, the affirmations simply assert what the Christian believes in faith, namely, that in Christ all things are one and that the Total Christ is ever-growing in health, wholeness and holiness through the workings of the Holy Spirit.

Sacred Kything for Non-Christians

For those believers who are not Christian, we suggest a very simple alternative for making your kything sacred. The three steps are affirmed as follows:

(1) When you have gotten centered and are present to yourself, say aloud or to yourself, **"I am alive in God."** Picture yourself, for example, surrounded by a circle of divine light.

(2) When you are focused lovingly on the other person and holding them in an image, say to them in spirit, **"You are alive in God."** You may picture the other person held lovingly by God in a circle of light.

(3) When you establish an image that connects you with the other person, perhaps picturing the two circles of light bringing the two of you together, choose the union by saying to the other in spirit, **"Together we are one in God."**

Redefining Reality

For Christians, indwelling in Christ fundamentally redefines reality. "You are all baptized in Christ, and have clothed yourselves in Christ, and there are no more distinctions between Jew and Greek, slave and free, male and female, but *all of you are one* in Christ Jesus" (Gal 3:27–28).

At the level of spirit and soul we are all equals. Whenever you kythe with another it is from a position of equality and reciprocity. In kything you are always a receiver as well as a giver, a learner as well as a teacher, loved as well as loving.

Because of this mutual indwelling, physical and material standards are changed. "From now on, we do not judge anyone by the standards of the flesh. Even if we did once know Christ in the flesh, that is not how we know him now. For anyone who is *in* Christ, there is a new creation [i.e., the whole universe has been re-created by Christ and lives *in* Christ]. The old creation has gone, and now the new one is here [i.e., everything is new]" (2 Cor 5:16–17).

"The proof that you are sons and daughters is that God has sent the Spirit of his Son *into our hearts*" (Gal 4:6). The Galatians are not slaves any longer but are sons and daughters of God. When they showed signs of slipping back into their ways of slavery again, Paul exclaimed, "I must go through the pain of giving birth to you all over again, until Christ is formed *in* you" (Gal 4:20). No matter how often you forget who you are in Christ, said Paul, you are invited to choose the indwelling once again. By kything, you may affirm your union with Christ again and again, and with all the sons and daughters of God. Indwelling may be developed, deepened, and intensified through kything.

Indwelling is also seen as the condition of resurrection of the Christian. In the Letter to the Romans we read, "Though your body may be dead it is because of sin, but if Christ is *in* you then your spirit is life itself because you have been justified; and if the Spirit of him who raised Jesus from the dead is living *in* you, then he who raised Jesus from the dead will give life to your own mortal bodies through his Spirit living *in* you" (Rom 8:10–11). It follows that, when we are living *in* Christ, there is nothing in the universe that is unreachable through kything.

Permanent and Continuous Indwelling

Clearly the Johannine and Pauline traditions highlight the experience of a permanent and continuous indwelling of us in the Christ and in the Father, and of the Spirit of the Father and the Christ indwelling in us.

Kything is a form of relating that produces spiritual oneness since it connects people center-to-center, or soul-to-soul. When Jesus says, "I live *in* the Father and the Father lives *in* me" or "I and the Father are one," he is describing a unity based on a kind of kything presence. In our language, Jesus asserted that he and his Father were in a permanent kythe.

The purpose of indwelling among Jesus, the Father, and all believers is to build an active and permanent relationship of loving unity and spiritual oneness: "That they may be one as we are one—I living *in* them, you living *in* me—that their oneness may be complete" (Jn 17:22–23). In this context we can more fully understand Paul's paradoxical cry of joy: "I live, now not I; but Christ lives *in* me" (Gal 2:20). When Christ lives *in* you, he brings with him all of reality, and kything gives you direct spiritual access to all reality in Christ.

Indwelling and Identity

It is well to note that the oneness of indwelling is a special kind of unity that does not destroy anyone's individuality or uniqueness, not even that of Jesus. Just as Jesus asserts, "I and the Father are one" (Jn 10:30), he asserts just as strongly that he and his Father are distinct persons and in fact even qualify as legally distinct persons (Jn 8:16).

We are created to find our true uniqueness and individuality in relationships. The more spiritually we become one with each other in a healthy union of souls, the more clearly we discover who we truly are. In this sense, by kything with others and with Christ you are developing your unique power and personality in loving ways.

178

Kything also helps you recognize and reverence the uniqueness of the person with whom you kythe. In step 2 of the kything process, you focus on the other person in a spirit of unconditional love, and you are able to see them without the biases of your expectations of them. "The other is no longer fashioned in my image and I begin to perceive the *core* of the other, enabling me to transcend my thoughts, images and concepts," explains Teresa Boersig. Sometimes it is rather painful to give up the strings we attach to and the expectations we place upon others as the conditions of our loving them. "Love always urges us to explore further into the mystery we do not understand. It is in this purgation—the pain of allowing the other to be other—that we become vulnerable to the other."[9]

Kything changes the focus in relating. When I kythe I don't force you to play the role I want you to play for me; instead I become real myself and make the gift of my uniqueness and your uniqueness available to both of us.

Energized Through Indwelling

For Jesus, mutual indwelling also has to do with energy and action. Jesus counts on sharing energies when he is consciously spiritually present to the Father. "The words I speak are not spoken of myself," says Jesus; "it is the Father who lives *in* me accomplishing his works" (Jn 14:10). In a similar way, through his indwelling in his followers, Jesus passes on to them the glory he is given by his Father (Jn 17:22) and he energizes us to speak and act *by means of his energies.* "If you live *in* me and my words stay part of you, you may ask what you will—it will be done for you" (Jn 15:7).

As you already know from earlier chapters, you may use the kything process to call upon the gifts and energies of those with whom you kythe.

During the persecution of the Christians in the second century the Carthaginian slave girl, Felicitas, described kything with Jesus and the energy she felt from that presence and union. When the jailers asked her how she

---

[9]Teresa Boersig, "Seven Mansions, Prayer and Relationship," *Review for Religious,* January 1981, p. 84 and p. 86.

planned to endure the pain of being chewed alive by the beasts, she replied, "Another will be *in* me who will suffer for me, as I shall suffer for him."

The kind of spiritual communion among people made possible by kything seems central to the living *in* each other—the indwelling—that is so important in Jesus' teaching and prayer. For Jesus, living *in* each other, *in* him, and *in* the Father was the summit of loving, the fulfillment of his single new commandment "to love one another as I have loved you" (Jn 13:34). Jesus showed his love by indwelling in his friends, making his spiritual home *in* them. In turn, he wanted his friends to love each other by co-inhering in each other as well as in him. Ultimately for the Christian, to kythe lovingly is to participate in the divine life; it is to form a oneness with Jesus and the Father.

Kything with Christ

The Jesus who walked and talked on our planet in the first century is no longer walking and teaching in the human body he received from Mary. The Jesus who lives today is the risen Christ in whom we all live as in a great Christ-Body. "I am the vine; you are the branches. Whoever remains *in* me, with me *in* him, bears fruit in plenty" (Jn 15:5). Insofar as we have chosen to be connected to Christ (i.e., to belong to the Christ-Body) and are committed to his commandment of love for each other, we live *in* him and he lives *in* us, individually and collectively.

When we kythe with Christ we become consciously spiritually present to the Christ who is alive today. And because Christ carries his human history with him forever (just as we do), we may kythe with him at any moment of his divine or human life, past, present, and future. We may kythe with him as Word of God in the depths of eternity before time began; as the Wisdom of God in the days of creation; as the infant child born on Christmas Day; as the preacher and healer who worked in Judea and Galilee; as the Son now living in the bosom of the Father; as the Total Christ living in each of the branches of his vine. By kything with Christ during meditation, we can re-experience *in* him any of the events of his temporal or eternal existence.

Beginning Prayer with Kything

Ignatius Loyola recommends that before each period of formal prayer or worship you place yourself in the presence of Christ. Of course, Christ is always present to you. Your task is to become consciously aware of this divine presence. When you do this at the beginning of your prayer, it enhances your devotion and makes you conscious of your life *in* Christ.

In his *Spiritual Exercises* when he gives directions for preparing to pray, Ignatius Loyola comes close to describing kything. In "Some Additional Directions" for the retreatant, he writes of becoming consciously spiritually present to God.

> A step or two from the place where I am going to meditate or contemplate, I will stand for the space of an "Our Father," and with my mind raised on high, I will consider that God our Lord sees me, etc. And I will make an act of reverence or humility.

Despite all the details of where and when to stand and for how long, Ignatius does not tell us step-by-step how to become spiritually present to God or to Christ. In fact, the presence described here is not quite mutual. "God our Lord sees me," but there is no mention of my "seeing" God. Later on, in suggestions for meditations and contemplations, Ignatius encourages us to converse with God the Father and with Christ, but there is no clear sense of an indwelling relationship.

Knowing the steps in the kything process can enhance the Ignatian experience of being in the presence of God or Christ.

To consciously kythe with Christ, for example, follow the three steps suggested above: First, take the time to get centered; kything can hardly happen if you are "somewhere else" and not centered within yourself. Say, **I am present to myself.**

Second, focus on Christ and let him become the object of your thought; here, Ignatius' advice—"with my mind raised on high, I will consider that God our Lord [or in this case, Christ] sees me, etc."—may be helpful. Alternatively, you might like to choose the moment in Christ's life

181

that you would like to experience during your prayer and picture Christ in your imagination at that moment in time; you may also choose or petition for the gift or grace you would like to have as a result of the kything union. When you have an image of the divine presence say, **I am present to your Spirit.**

Third, consciously acknowledge some existing connection between you and Christ; to facilitate this, create an image of you and Christ connected in some way (e.g., you as a branch connected to his vine) and affirm the union you are imaging. Say, **I live in you and you live in me.**

In his book *The Spiritual Exercises,* Ignatius offered images of being connected with Christ, but because he lived in an age of chivalry he often chose images that emphasized a superior-inferior union between him and Christ, e.g., Christ as King and himself as obedient knight, or Christ as Lord of the castle and himself as a lowly slave or servant. In our age of freedom and equality, we tend to create images of Christ as friend or brother. Find the images that work best for you and use them.

The primary purpose of using an image is to help you find your way into a kythe. Without losing any reverence for Christ, kything emphasizes not the distance between you and Christ but the closeness, intimacy, and co-creativity to which you are being invited by Christ. He has after all chosen to dwell in you permanently. Kything makes you aware of the familiarity you have with Christ and your continual access and availability to him. He is hardly a "guest" in your soul, for he is at home there. The truth is that your spirit is his home—and his Spirit is your home.

If you kythe with Christ during a period of prayer or worship, maintain the spiritual communion as long as you wish, using imagery to help you keep your attention focused on your mutual presence. At the end of formal prayer or worship, consciously bring the kythe with Christ to an end and go back to your work. To bring kything to an end merely means you cease being *consciously* focused upon Christ's presence. The underlying permanent mutual indwelling that you enjoy by being a member of the Christ Body never ceases, even though you don't consciously think of it.

A Colloquy with Christ

It is valuable to kythe with Christ at the outset of prayer. If you do, your prayer time is bound to be more intense, confident, and loving, and you will undoubtedly feel a closer sense of the divine presence. A kind of dia-logue—or "colloquy" as Ignatius calls it—may also spontaneously occur during the period of prayer, though do not expect that it must take the form of words and sentences. While such formal conversation is possible and reported by many who have kythed with Christ, more likely the dia-logue will happen at the level of symbols, images, colors, and sensations. Christ's touch might be felt as a sense of warmth, or a tingling in the skin, especially at the fingers and toes. Do not pre-define or limit the possible ways Christ can commune and communicate with you.

Kything with Christ Outside of Formal Prayer

In addition to kything with Christ during periods of formal prayer and worship, you may also kythe with him at many other times: whenever you are about to enter a situation that seems dangerous, threatening, scary, tempting or evil (e.g., when you must deal with a person who is angry at you, or who doesn't like you, or who has been cruel to you, or who is closed off to you); in the hospital before surgery, or when waiting for someone who is having surgery; when going on a long drive alone, especially if you feel frightened or do not know your way; when you want to celebrate something wonderful and joyful that has happened to you or to someone you love; at family celebrations such as Christmas or Easter, a birthday or an anniversary; when doing dreamwork on dreams that are confusing, complex or make you feel anxious; at grace before meals. In each of these situations, take a moment to carry out the three basic steps: Get centered, focus on Christ, then establish a connection with him.

19. Kything and
The Communion of Saints

A Common Love

As long as all of us who are children of God and comprise one family in Christ remain in communion with one another in mutual love and in praising God, we are responding to our highest vocation and partaking in a foretaste of the experience of divine glory.

In the Final Day of glory, the human race as well as the entire universe, which is intimately related to us and achieves its purpose through us, will be perfectly re-established in Christ (Eph 1:10; Col 1:20; 2 Pet 3:10–13). Christ "will refashion the body of our lowliness, conforming it to the body of his glory" (Phil 3:21). He will be "glorified in his saints and to be marveled at in all those who have believed" (2 Thes 1:10). This promised restoration has already begun in Christ and is being carried forward by the Holy Spirit in all of us. A common love urges us to live for all the members of the Body of Christ (2 Cor 5:15), and to please the Lord in all things (2 Cor 5:9).

In this common love, available to conscious experience through kything, we are willing to put ourselves in another's place, to suffer for them, to console them, to rejoice with them, in a word, to live *in* them.

In the third century Clement of Alexandria meditating on Christ's love saw its essence as that of *exchange and substitution.* "For the sake of each of us Christ laid down his life—worth no less than the universe. He demands of us in return our lives for the sake of each other."

And in the following century the hermit Macarius of Egypt renowned for his miracles and counsel advised the monk Arsenius to develop his ability for coinherence or indwelling:

> It is right for a man to take up the burden of them that are near to him, whatever it may be, and, so to speak, to put his own soul in the place of that of his neighbor, and to become, if it were possible, a double man; and he must suffer and weep and mourn with the other person. And finally the matter must be accounted by him as if he himself had put on the actual body of his neighbor, and as if he had acquired the other's countenance and soul, and he must suffer for him as he would for himself. For thus it is written *We are all one body,* and this passage also informs us concerning the holy and mysterious kiss.[1]

All who belong to Christ, having his Spirit, form one community and cleave together *in* him (Eph 4:16). Because we live *in* Christ, our love for one another does not stop at the grave no more than Christ's love stopped at his grave. The union that we, the wayfarers who are still on our earthly journey, have with those who have gone to sleep in the peace of Christ is not the least interrupted. On the contrary, that bond is strengthened through the exchange of spiritual goods. For, just as communion among fellow believers brings us closer to Christ, so our companionship with the saints in heaven joins us to Christ, from whom issues every grace and the very life of God's people. As one of our students put it,

> To imagine a network of spirits available to me in my own development, available to the planet in its evolution, is compatible with my understanding of God as one who wastes nothing, but instead transforms all things yielding to him. Intercessory prayer and sacrifice, spiritual disciplines which I have practiced but never under-

---

[1] Sad to say, we are no longer able to find the source of this quotation. It was transcribed a few years ago, but the citation's source was omitted.

stood, all came alive through kything with new depths of meaning.

In Christ, it is just as easy to kythe with someone on the other side of life as with someone on the other side of town. Whether you need support or rejoicing, whether you need to renew your energies or feel an overflow of creativity, whether you need to confront an angry friend or show love to an older person, there is someone in the communion of saints who is eager to kythe with you in order to be of help to you.

The communion of saints is primarily a mutual interchange and interplay of energies and gifts, help and prayer, support and good works among all the members of the Body of Christ. Whether those members are alive or have died on earth, each of them is alive *in* Christ. All of us come together to form one Living City whose governor is Christ and whose law is unconditional love. The common life that Christians share with Christ and the Father in their one Spirit (Eph 2:18) leads of itself to a sharing of life (*koinonia*) among all those who have been given life by the same Spirit. Among Christ's members there exists a most varied inward-outward interplay of new life, a network of connections whose interchanges flow with energies and gifts, helps and services of all forms.[2]

Each One's Contribution to the Christ-Body

"Just as each of our bodies has several parts and each part has a separate function, so all of us in Christ form one body, and as parts of it we belong to each other" (Rom 12:4–5). The emphasis here is on member's solidarity and vital interdependence—a sharing of goods and life. When we share in the trials and sufferings of each other, it brings into play a communion in suffering within the Body of Christ that works to the good of the

---

[2]See Phlm 17; Rom 12:13, 15:26–27; 2 Cor 8:4, 9:13; Phil 4:14–20; Gal 6:6; Heb 13:16; Acts 2:42.

whole.[3] The purpose of this interchange of life is for the "building up of the Body of Christ" (Eph 4:12).

This body of believers forms a dynamic unity *in* Christ. This body in its truest being is both a shared destiny and a shared existence with each other *in* Christ. *The fundamental law of the Body of Christ is the intercommunion among its members.* By gifting themselves to Christ the members of the Body enable him dwelling in them to avail himself of the unique riches of their myriad personal existences and gifts in order to complete, qualitatively and quantitatively, the work of the incarnation and redemption.

In Christ, the Father has brought us into the sphere of divine life (Jn 14:6–24; 1 Jn 2:23, 5:11–13) and given us communion with himself and his Son (1 Jn 1:1–3; 1 Cor 1:9). The members who receive this gift of life and its benefits will tend to be like Christ their head, who "lives always to make intercession" (Heb 7:25). The ardent concern of Christians on earth is the spread of God's kingdom. This concern is intensified among the saints in heaven because they understand with greater clarity the spiritual needs of those on earth. For this reason, they become advocates and protectors of us on earth, interceding for us. Thus, between the heavenly saints and those on earth there is established a bond of confident intimacy, like that existing between older and younger family members. This bond in no way diminishes the greatness of Christ or the unique relationship to Christ and with God that each believer enjoys. Rather it enriches and deepens them, just as does every act of love among the members.

It was a consistent practice in the early Church to ask those who died in Christ to intercede on behalf of the living. And there is a harvest of evidence concerning the faith and conviction in such intercessory power of the saints found in epitaphs, anaphorae, litanies of the saints, liturgical documents, writings of the martyrs, and patristic literature. For example, on an ancient tombstone we read, "Gerantius, a faithful one, now in peace, who lived 21 years, 8 months, and 16 days, intercede for us by your prayers because we know you are in Christ."

---

[3]See Col 1:24; 2 Cor 4:12–15; 1:5–7.

Kything with the Saints

Our daily prayers offer us simple and frequent ways to participate in this network of spiritual presence, affirm it, be grateful for it, and develop it.

Whenever you pray to Mary the mother of Jesus or to other saints, you presume that they are spiritually available to you, that they "hear" your prayer. Kything consciously focuses on this availability and offers a way to explicitly connect with the presence of the holy ones to whom you pray. Kythe with the saints using the three basic steps of the process: Get yourself centered, focus on the saint with whom you want to kythe, and establish a connection with the saint using appropriate imagery and choosing the union.

The saints are open to communion with us and willing to intercede or to share their gifts and experiences with us. They want us to become everything we can be and to live to our highest potential.

One woman in our workshop reported kything with a team of saints. (She had been doing this for years, but never had a name for it.) Among her team were Thomas Aquinas, Thomas More, and Julian of Norwich. Whenever she had a problem she would kythe with her team using them as an executive board, returning to them again and again until they helped her find a solution. "I chose these particular saints for their wisdom," she explained.

We often ask people learning to kythe for the first time to begin kything with their favorite saint, since it is most likely that such a connection will be easy and successful. People are more likely to continue practicing kything when they are successful at it.

Also, when you are trying to kythe with someone who may be emotionally closed-off to you, kythe first with your favorite saint (or with the other person's favorite saint); saints are good at being go-betweens. When one woman was unable to establish a kythe directly with her daughter (apparently the daughter was resentful of her mother), she first kythed with St. Catherine of Siena whom the daughter admired, and then together the mother and the saint kythed easily with the daughter.

The Unfinished Work of the Saints

For saints, having arrived safely in heaven does not mean they have finished growing or that their loving service has come to an end. Far from it. The Communion of Saints is not a retirement home, but a network of actively involved members of the Body of Christ. From their vantage point saints can see better than we do what needs to be done to build up the Body of Christ on earth.

Furthermore, in order for the great work of Christ to be accomplished on earth, the saints (who see the tasks still waiting to be done) need our help in fulfilling their own service. It is very narrow-minded to think that you or I have nothing to offer Saint Francis or Saint Ignatius or Saint Teresa. The communion available to the Christ-members in kything is not a one-sided event. We humans underestimate our value to the Body of Christ when we think that the saints are always the givers and we always the receivers.

To test this we asked our workshop participants to kythe with their favorite saint and to ask that saint for a gift. "Then," we added, "see if your saint would like a gift from you." The participants were pleasantly surprised to discover that the saints with whom they kythed consistently asked for gifts.

One woman asked from Peter the Apostle the gift of authenticity and spontaneity, which he gladly shared with her. Peter in turn wanted from her an ability which she had, to listen sensitively.

From both Teresa of Avila and Catherine of Siena another woman asked for wisdom in leadership. They in turn asked her to give them a sense of contemporary women in the Church.

Sometimes the gifts exchanged with saints are symbolic and require reflection and discernment to discover their meanings. A nun who does counseling kythed with the foundress of her order, Mother Marie of Providence, and after asking for a gift received a crystal figurine, a hand with a bird in its palm. (Later in the workshop someone, unaware of the nun's kything experience, gave her a print of a hand with a bird in it. The nun found this a wonderful confirmation of her kything experience.) When during the kything the foundress had asked for a gift in return, the nun found herself spontaneously giving the saint a basket full of crystals, each representing one of her clients. The saint was evidently delighted with the gift. (We never heard what the hand with the bird in it symbolized.)

Times for Kything with Saints

Here are some suggestions for kything with the saints.

Most people have a favorite holy person or patron saint. You may have even read biographies of these saints or books they wrote. Kything allows you to go a step beyond knowing "about" the saint; it gives you a chance to be connected to the saint spirit-to-spirit.

If you find you need special graces or gifts to accomplish some task, kythe with a saint who has the qualities or energies you need and ask for help. Invite the saint to contribute the gifts you need and to be actively present *in* you as you do the task.

One of our workshop participants, a devout, middle-aged man who felt very much at home within the Communion of Saints, had never thought of establishing a kything network with saints to help a member of his family who needed reconciliation. The prayer-in-kything experience he described was filled with comfortable, everyday imagery and places familiar to him and his family. As you will see, in kythe he was able to move the focus of his spirit quickly and easily. The entire experience happened within his spirit and took less than five minutes of clock-time.

I traveled with the Blessed Mother and St. Dominic to a daughter of mine in the Mid-West, and after a discussion with her there, the four of us came home to our family in Connecticut and together we discussed our need for reconciliation with our daughter. Blessed Mother was the one who did most of the talking to her in the Mid-West, and St. Dominic spoke to her as we met in our kitchen at home. He had her promise to work toward reconciliation with all of us at home, including her mother and me, her four sisters and her brother. The realization of how the Communion of

Saints works with us in this way impressed me and consoled me for the entire weekend.

You might also like to share special moments of joy in your life by taking a saint along with you in kythe.

You may kythe with saints for their wisdom and understanding. For example, many people find the writings of Pierre Teilhard de Chardin especially difficult to comprehend. Before reading one of his books, kythe with him and ask that you be able to understand what you read by being present *in* him. In general, before reading a book kythe with its author—not simply to comprehend the meaning of the words but also to feel the author's energy and motivation.

In this same light, when listening to the biblical readings at church or when reading a certain book of the Bible, kythe with the author before you begin. When you are in communion with St. Paul, for example, you will begin to understand what he wrote *from within his spirit.* You may be surprised at the new depth of meaning you experience when reading the sacred books.

In the Christian tradition Mary the mother of Jesus has always been the most popular of all the saints. Kythe with Mary who suffered with her son when you seem to lack the strength to deal lovingly with family trauma, disagreements, separations, death, and sickness. Kythe with Mary if you want to develop your feminine qualities and your freedom to choose. Kythe with her when you need the energy to say "yes" to your destiny and to remain true to yourself. Kythe with Mary in all things having to do with childbirth. And kythe with her whenever you sing or pray with words that refer to her.

It has been a consistent Christian belief that there are angels, spiritual beings who complement the kingdom of God and who, like the saints, want to do all they can to bring about the fulfillment of Christ's work on earth. Traditionally, the task of the angels has been that of guardians, protectors, and messengers. For example, each of us is assured that we have an angel to guard us and to lead us safely along the right path. It would be very natural to kythe with such a spirit guide and to establish a conscious relationship with it as you would with any lifelong companion.

These suggestions are not something crazy. True, such kything experiences are not verifiable in physical or psychological reality, though sometimes in minor miraculous moments such verification might happen—as when the woman gave the nun in the workshop a print of a hand holding a bird, the same image she had seen earlier in kythe with her foundress. But the spiritual realm of itself is very real, despite the fact that many people stay away from it or at least avoid acknowledging its reality. Kything provides a simple and structured way to begin exploring consciously this non-ordinary but natural dimension of life. It is an exciting exploration. The more you explore the world of the sacred, the more you will feel at home in it. Remember, you are always *in* Christ, no matter where or with whom you kythe.

Kything with a Beloved Person Who Has Died

One of the most consoling aspects of kything is its ability to transcend death. Since the soul of the person who has passed from this life is still very much alive in Christ, it is possible to be in communion with that soul. (Souls contain all the history and life-experience of that person, their values and choices, their loves and commitments, etc. Therefore, souls are not abstract, undefined entities but uniquely personal ones. It is of the nature of the soul to be in relationship to other souls, since its primary energy is love and its primary purpose is union and communion.)

People want spontaneously to be in touch with the souls of their family and friends who have died. Some of us have unanswered questions we would like to pose to them. Some of us have something we wanted to say but never did. Most of us simply want to enjoy again, in whatever ways possible, the presence of the person who has departed because he or she is missed.

One elderly woman whose husband had died six months before continued to walk around the family farm after supper as she used to do every evening with her husband when he was still alive. She missed having him at her side now, though she confessed rather embarrassedly that at times it felt as though he was still at her side. When we suggested that he probably *was* present and that she could kythe with her husband's soul each night during her walk—and share her feelings and possibly converse with him in her heart while she was in this state of communion—she was most grateful. Primarily she was grateful because we had told her that she was not crazy, that spiritual communion was possible, that there was a name and a formula for the experience she enjoyed so much, and that the steps for doing kything were extremely simple. What we said only confirmed that what she felt at times was indeed more than a figment of her imagination, and might indeed be her husband seeking a kythe. Now she could consciously accept his invitation to kythe when it occurred, or she herself could initiate a kythe with him at any time.

In Christ we are all already joined in communion. At the level of spirit we experience this communion, even though our conscious egos are frequently unaware of the experience.

Allaying Fears About Kything with Those Who Have Died

Some years ago, the Episcopalian Bishop James Pike lost his son through suicide. In prayer the bishop reported that his son "visited" him and said that he was in an in-between place and asking for help. The description the son gave sounded a lot like what in the Catholic tradition is called purgatory, a state of purification. It is often pictured as a cleansing fire (not to be confused with the "fires" of hell). Those in purgatory are *in* Christ; they are members of the Body of Christ and able to enjoy the exchanges of love and energy available to all the members.

Some people express apprehension about kything with such souls. They may fear that kything with those who have died, like Bishop Pike's experience of communion with his son, is reminiscent of midnight seances and mediums conjuring up souls from the dead. There is no need for such fear. Kything has nothing to do with spiritualism or the occult. If you chose to associate in love and friendship with these persons when they were physically alive, there is no reason to believe that kything with them after their death would be harmful in any way. Usually, like Bishop Pike's son, these are the souls we would most want to help and support. And kything with them in an intercessory way is a very loving thing to do.

It is likely that some souls of the dead, perhaps like Bishop Pike's son, have certain unresolved issues, which is why they are in an in-between place and asking for help. Some may still be harboring resentment, hatred, jealousy, pride, etc., and be unable to forgive themselves or others. Such souls are also being confronted with the purifying light of God's love and so are more intent on working through the issues keeping them from total communion with God rather than intensifying their pride or hatred.

Kything with such souls would not in any way contradict the traditional teaching and practice of the Church to pray for them, but would add a new dimension to that prayer. Kything with them would intensify the loving bond that exists between the living and the dead and the communion among all the members of the Body of Christ. It would also help build conscious links between the various dimensions of the Total Christ.

It is possible, though not probable, that you might attempt to kythe with a person whose total orientation is toward the destruction of peace, love, relationship, and communion. As far as we can tell, such a spirit would not welcome your peaceful and loving kythe, but would be closed to it. You would not be able to effect a kythe since the other soul would not be willing to enter the Body of Christ in which you live and move.

On the other hand, if such a hypothetical spirit tried to initiate a connection with you, your spirit would spontaneously reject such an invitation. Love is the only key that can open the door to the center of your being; a spirit with evil intention cannot possess such a key. Except for God, no force in heaven or on earth can overpower your free will, the assent of your innermost being which lives in God. God alone can touch your soul uninvited.

For those who would like to try kything but remain hesitant about connecting spirit-to-spirit with certain deceased persons, it might be helpful first to kythe with Jesus, Mary or another saint. Then, while connected to and protected by the holy person, you may proceed to kythe with any other soul. Some report that when they first kythe with a saint, the saint introduces them to the soul of the person departed, so that the union right from the start feels relaxed and familiar.

Suggestions for Kything with the Deceased

To help establish a kythe with those who have died, use the same three basic steps outlined in Chapter 2. We suggest you imagine the union happening in some place or situation you both shared on earth. You may also help keep yourself focused on the kythe by looking at a photo or symbol of the deceased one.

Some people prefer to kythe with the dead during times of worship. Catholics often have Masses celebrated in honor of the deceased person as a way of interceding for them. Kything with such souls at worship for their benefit is most appropriate.

If you have unfinished business or unresolved issues with someone who has died, you might try kything on a long drive or when you are alone or in some other place where you won't be disturbed. Imagine the person sitting on the seat beside you. (Remember, images simply help you to enter the kythe and maintain it; there is no need to believe that someone physically appears next to you.) When the kything relationship is established, say what you want to say or ask the questions you want to ask. Then wait. Get a sense of the response that comes. The response may not come in words (though it might), but rather in a sense of peace or forgiveness or something that directly touches your soul.

20. Kything and Liturgy

Presence at the Liturgy

We are not used to thinking about spiritual presence. In the Roman Catholic Church before Vatican Council II, only *physical presence* in church on Sundays was required by Canon Law. People faithfully brought themselves physically to church, but since the liturgy was conducted in Latin many people did not understand fully what was going on. Consequently, their psychological attention wandered far away from the pew where their body was sitting. Except during the sermon, there was little or no communication expected to happen between priest and people.

To change that sad state of affairs, the documents of Vatican II encouraged *psychological presence* by requiring that the Latin language be dropped in liturgical services in favor of the vernacular. This was an attempt to help people comprehend and consciously participate in what was going on at the church services. The new liturgy was designed to include dialogue between priest and people, and communication began to grow.

Even with the new liturgical requirements, however, *spiritual presence* remained underdeveloped. Conscious spiritual communion among priest, people, and God was still often a missing ingredient in the liturgy. Although people had always been encouraged to be reverent and devout at Mass, few liturgical leaders knew ways to teach people how to be spiritually present to the sacred events happening before their eyes. Even years after Vatican II, few leaders had developed the skills to show people how to add the dimension of spirit-to-spirit presence to their worship: *how* to become one with God, *how* to participate actively in the Communion of Saints, *how* to be spiritually present to the celebrant and the other worshipers, etc.

Christian doctrines tell us that at the liturgy we are in fact in the presence of God and in communion with the angels and saints. The liturgical text reminds us that the angelic hosts as well as the entire court of heaven are all spiritually present to us witnessing our worship. For example, one Preface prayer ends with the words, "And so *we join the angels and saints* in proclaiming your glory as we say, Holy, Holy, Holy . . ." and another Preface ends, "Countless hosts of angels stand before you . . . *united with them* . . . we too praise your glory as we say, Holy, Holy, Holy . . . " Even though people may hear the liturgical words affirming such spiritual presence, they are seldom instructed *how* to become conscious of this presence, how to develop it, intensify it, focus it, enrich it, and use it creatively.

The ability to consciously create and participate in spiritual presence or communion is an art that needs to be learned and practiced, just as good communication is an art that needs to be learned and practiced. Kything provides a technique for being actively and consciously present to the sacred events at a spiritual level.

Kything and the Eucharist

The eucharistic liturgy which Catholics call the Mass is the highpoint of worship in the Christian community, because it is a locus where the entire Body of Christ is intentionally gathered. In this setting the risen Jesus Christ, the Head of the Body, manifests himself in a special way, as he did at the Last Supper when he blessed the bread and wine and said, "This is my body . . . This is my blood." The ritual of receiving Holy Communion from the consecrated bread and wine is a special expression of the mutual indwelling of Christ in the believers and the believers in Christ.

Insofar as the sacred bread and wine make present the Christ who lives today—the Total Christ, head and members—the believer who receives the sacrament receives the Total Christ who lives today, and thus in receiving

197

Holy Communion experiences the mutual indwelling of all the members of Christ.

So, in the eucharistic liturgy you experience the central reality of the Christian life: Christ in you, you in Christ, each and all of the other members in you, and you in each and all of the other members—a comprehensive co-inherence.

Kything Before the Liturgy

Kything can help make this awesome experience more conscious and concrete. Here are a few suggestions for using kything before the liturgy.

Before the service begins, take a few minutes to grow centered so that you can enter into the kything process fully and deeply.

You might want to begin by kything with one or more of the people sitting in the congregation, especially those who might not seem attractive to you. This will challenge you to view them—and be present to them—at the spirit-to-spirit level.

You may kythe with the angels and saints (sometimes it's easier simply to kythe with a few specific ones) imagining them, for example, hovering above the congregation.

You may also kythe with believers who are attending worship at this moment in different parts of the world.

You may kythe with persons whom you wish would be, or could be, with you at this liturgy, e.g., a friend who is away on a trip, a friend who is troubled or ill, a family member or person with whom you are having difficulty, even someone who has died.

If you do no other kything than one of the above, you will find yourself deeply present to the worship.

Before Mass begins, one man kythes with all his children (who are all grown and living in various parts of the country). A woman kythes with her husband who has, as they say, "fallen away from the Church." A woman recently widowed kythes with her deceased husband.

Ask yourself whom you would like to have in your heart during the service; then kythe with that person or persons.

Kything During the Liturgy

When the Bible is being read, kythe with the readers so that they might read the word of God with the spirit of the author. Or kythe with the writer of the sacred text, whether it is Saint Paul, Mark, Matthew, Luke or John, so that you might understand the meaning of the Scripture passages in a deeply personal way.

Kythe with the celebrant of the Eucharist during the sermon and during the more important liturgical moments. Picture Christ in kythe with the celebrant. Envision them side by side, inside one another, or coinhering.

When the celebrant addresses the congregation with the affirmation, "The Lord be with you," take a moment to acknowledge God's presence and indwelling in you.

When the celebrant says, "May the peace of Christ be with you," acknowledge the truth of the blessing. And when you greet your neighbors with "Peace be with you," take a moment to let your "peace" (flowing from your spirit) flow into them and kythe with them if only momentarily.

At the offering of the gifts of bread and wine you may analogously kythe with the bread and wine. Those gifts are meant to symbolize you and the other believers; the offering is your offering to God of yourselves. In turn, Christ will kythe with the bread and wine and co-inhere in them. In kything with the bread and wine you are ready and eager for the Christ to come and fill you and the world once again with his divine life.

After receiving Holy Communion use kything to help you remain conscious of the coinhering event that is taking place. It is a time when you may call upon the entire Christ Body to help you create what you most deeply want to create in your life and in your part of the planet, what you most essentially want to be.

Carol's dearest friend Eleanor is an alcoholic who cannot drink wine at Holy Communion but would really like to be able to. So, when it is Communion time both the women kythe with each other as they receive the consecrated bread; then Carol "receives" the wine *in* Eleanor. When she kythes, Carol images her lips, tongue, teeth, and throat merged with those of Eleanor, and Eleanor does the same. Eleanor "tastes" the wine *in* Carol.

It is a powerful experience for both of them. The moment of "not receiving" the sacred wine, instead of reminding Eleanor that she is an alcoholic, has become an action that strengthens their bond of friendship and their oneness in Christ.

The eucharistic liturgy is a cosmic spiritual event. Instead of remaining a passive spectator in it, use kything to help you actively participate in the worship and to help bring the Body of Christ one step closer to its fullest maturity.

If you cannot be present at the liturgy but would like to be, kythe with someone who is present. Visualize yourself in the church pew, kneeling next to the person with whom you are kything. Thanks to kything, there is never a need to spiritually "miss" an important sacred event.

Kything and Prayer

"Where two or three are gathered in my name, I shall be there with them" (Mt 18:20). When you pray, begin by kything with someone special. By kything with a friend or a saint you can always make sure there are two or three gathered in the name of Christ. Kythe with someone who is absent—one of your children, a spouse, a parent, a friend. Kythe with your favorite holy person or spiritual teacher. Kythe with someone in the world who, like you, is at prayer at this moment.

When you wish to pray for someone who is sick, kythe with the sick person beforehand. It will intensify your prayer and bless him or her with your spiritual presence. If you wish to pray for someone who is in temptation or who has sinned, kythe with him or her before you pray to God. "We are quite confident that if we ask God for anything," wrote John, "and it is in accordance with his will, he will hear us. . . . If anybody sees his brother commit a sin . . . he has only to pray, and God will give life to the sinner" (1 Jn 5:14–15).

Kything may be used to develop social consciousness. During periods of prayer, kythe with persons who are poor, hungry, homeless, unemployed, battered, imprisoned, handicapped, forgotten, lonely, rejected, terminally ill, confined, disenfranchised, the victims of racial, sexual, social or religious prejudice. The power of the kythe may be intensified if you can specify images of the persons who need socially-conscious care and concern.

In this context the Lord's Prayer is meant to be a prayer of a community, since it begins with the plural "Our." Before saying the Lord's Prayer you might symbolically reach out with your arms in a gesture of union to all those—as specifically as possible—who are ill-treated by society (and therefore by you as part of society). Be willing to hold hands, spiritually, with each of them. In kything with this group of society's rejects, you will discover that the Lord's Prayer takes on a new and richer meaning for you.

Mystical prayer is essentially an experience of unity with God and God's creation. Kything is a gateway to mystical experience and can certainly foster deeper prayer states. When you kythe you transcend separateness without losing your identity. When you kythe you enter into a state of unconditional love and spiritual union.

Appendix:
Where and When Does Kything Happen?

The Locus of Kything

We humans are very physical beings. Places and times are very important to us. All the things we do, including our memories and our future plans, are associated with a date and a location. Even fantasy happens at a hypothetical time and place. "Once upon a time in the land of . . . " is how many of our fairy tales begin.

Even in theology we tend to talk about spiritual realities in the language of time and space. Heaven is described as a place and the way to it is upward; hell is viewed as a place, too, and the way to it is downward.

Perhaps the mind and certainly the imagination find it necessary to locate actions and events within the coordinates of time and space. For this reason kything usually gets talked about in time-space language. Though we know logically that the human spirit can operate outside the boundaries of time and space as well as within them, we still continue to talk about our souls and spirits as though they were governed and limited by those boundaries. Most of us spontaneously view our spirit as living within our skin.

In defining kything let us try to be as precise as we can, given the limitations of our language. Once we understand and agree on the "precise" meaning, we can relax and use more familiar time-space language for simplicity, knowing that we do so merely as a concession to human tendencies.

One of the first questions people ask is, "Where does kything happen?"

This is a question impossible to answer since kything does not happen in any *where.* It is a spiritual event. As such it transcends time and space, and cannot be localized. However, when I use my imagination to facilitate kything, the union will always be visualized as happening in a describable place—now within me, now within you, now outside us both. But your soul is not limited to your imagination's picture of it, no more than the taste of vanilla ice cream is limited by the words you use to describe it. Technically, since your soul is a spiritual entity, it is possible to say that it exists in every *where.* It embraces everything that is and every *where* that exists. In a very real sense, then, your soul is present at every moment to all that is. You may not be very conscious of the awesome length, breadth, depth, and height of your soul; it is likely you are usually aware of it only within the limits of your body.

A fact known to those who practice spiritual disciplines is that your soul or spirit can change its focus of presence, just as your mind can change its focus of attention. Just as a student's mind can in a moment change its attention from sociology to history, to literature or to lunch, so the soul can move the focus of its presence to any reality within the length and breadth of its scope. Such a change of soul-focus can happen within your body, as when you move the center of your awareness from your head to your heart, to your sexual organs, to your feet or to your hands, and back again. Each of us habitually centers our soul or spirit in some part of our body. My spirit may make its home within my head, while yours may make its home within your heart. Some people's spirits live life from their gut, while others' spirits operate primarily from their genitals as a source of power.

A simple way to tell what part of your body your soul calls home is to see how you react to a major experience of bad news. Do you respond with your intellect and try to find a solution? Do you respond with your heart and express emotions? Do you respond with your gut and clench up? Do you respond with your genitals and want to express your power? Once you learn to center yourself and notice where in your body your spirit tends to come to rest, you discover that you can move your center around and

203

even experiment what it feels like to be centered in different parts of your body. Kything seems to happen best when you are centered in your heart.

Such a change of soul-focus can also happen outside your body, for example, in Step 2 of kything when you move the center of your awareness to another person. Once you learn to get centered and to move the focus of your center within your body, you can also learn to move the focus of your soul's presence outside your body.

Does Your Soul Leave Your Body in Kything?

Some have asked us, "When you kythe, does your soul ever leave your body in order to enter another's body?"

The answer is "no." Since your soul itself is vaster than the planet, by definition your soul embraces your body as well as the other's body. What does change in kything is not your soul's position but *the focus of your soul's presence.* When you shift from being centered within yourself (Step 1) to centering on your kything partner (Step 2), your soul itself does not move, only its focus of presence. In a similar way, when you shift from studying sociology to history, your mind does not move from place to place, it merely changes its focus of attention.

Moreover, your mind does not lose the knowledge of sociology it has acquired the moment you switch your attention to your history assignment. Just as your mind embraces and holds simultaneously all the knowledge it has acquired, so your soul simultaneously embraces all the relationships and experiences it has accumulated consciously and unconsciously. When you take the time to get centered before kything (Step 1), your soul is focused upon you, and your imagination may picture your soul as being inside your body. When you then contemplate the other person (Step 2), your spiritual presence is focused outside your body, and your imagination may spontaneously picture your soul there. If you treat the imagination's symbolic images as a literal depiction of reality, then it may seem as though your soul has left your body. If imagery like this is troublesome to your sense of self, you can learn to use your imagination in such a way that it does not picture your soul as if it were leaving your body. Instead, you may image Steps 2 and 3 the way you would like them to be, for instance, you can picture both your soul and body and the soul and body of your partner sitting together somewhere, or being held in God's embrace, or walking together in some beautiful and peaceful scene.

Grammatically, we are forced to speak of the soul or spirit as a thing, since our language demands that we turn every experience we talk about into a noun or a verb. Clearly such parts of speech cannot precisely describe a soul or the experience of presence. However, since we settle for using a noun to describe the soul, we tend to treat it as a thing. And things are locatable in time and space and describable in time-and-space imagery. Thus, some people picture the soul as a mathematical point with no dimensions, yet which can locate itself at any coordinates in the four-dimensional time-space world. Others picture the soul as a ray of light emanating from a source deep within themselves and able to be aimed, like a laser beam, toward any object in the universe. Still others picture the soul as a little person, a miniaturized version of themselves which is free to move about or come to a stop anywhere in the universe. You may create images of your own to describe your soul and how it changes its focus of presence. Just remember, they are merely images that help you perform a spiritual action.

If it helps you to use such images to initiate a kythe, by all means use them as long as you do not restrict the dimensions of your soul to the limits set by your image of it. The mental image is merely a tool designed by the imagination to initiate or facilitate a spiritual event. When used for its intended purpose, having an image of your spirit or soul can be very helpful. When an image is proposed as an accurate description of spiritual reality, it can misrepresent the truth and distort what is really happening.

The Realm of Between

In what state of consciousness does kything happen? (This is a much better question than "Where does kything happen?")

It does not happen in the state of consciousness that we call "being centered" (Step 1), because in that state you are simply, though deeply, present to yourself.

It does not happen in the state of consciousness that we call "being single-focused" or "holding another in a contemplative gaze" (Step 2) because in that state you are merely focused on another person's spirit. In that state when your intended kything partner becomes the content of your mind and imagination, there is indeed a mental connection between you and the other person but it is not yet a connection of spirit-to-spirit presence.

Kything happens in a state of mutual presence, a state of betweenness. Strictly speaking, it happens neither in you nor in the other person, though to help foster the kythe you may *imagine* it happening within you or the other person.

What do you call this state of betweenness or this locus of mutual presence where kything happens? Martin Buber in his book, *I and Thou,* named this state the "Realm of Between." For him, the Realm of Between is where true relating happens and where real relationship lives.

A relationship between persons is a real entity, though not a physical one. A relationship, such as a marriage, is a spiritual entity which has its own life, its own history, its own birth, and its own strengths and weaknesses, which may be different from that of either of the partners in it. Our relationship does not exist in me or in you, though we are both affected by it. Rather, it exists *between* us.

When we step "into relationship," we step into the Realm of Between where relationships are born and grow. When I am truly present to you, my friend, and you to me, said Buber, the two of us shift into another realm of being (another state of consciousness, if you wish), a realm that transcends yet embraces my personal reality as well as the personal reality of my partner. This is the Realm of Between.

We enter this Realm of Between, said Buber, every time we enter into genuine dialogue with another (or with God), when we are truly and unconditionally open to whatever will happen between us. Unfortunately we seldom genuinely dialogue with others. We seldom come to a meeting open to a union of souls. More often we come, even to personal and intimate meetings, with an agenda to convince, to defend, to control, to get our own way, to complain or to release our feelings. We come self-programmed or attempting to program others. Instead of stepping into the Realm of Between when we come together, we remain inside ourselves.

To enter the Realm of Between, I must step out of the realm of my self-centered consciousness into another state, characterized by unconditional loving openness to others. I must be ready and open to whatever will happen without trying to plan, program or manipulate the spirit-to-spirit meeting and its outcome. What happens in the Realm of Between doesn't happen in me or in you, it happens *between* us. What happens between us affects both you and me. When we return to our personal realities after having been together spirit-to-spirit we are changed.

The Between is not emptiness. It is a spiritual realm where all relationship and love is born and nurtured. For Buber, it is the realm of dialogue. For us, it is the realm of communion, the communion of all being. The Christians call it the Communion of Saints.

We are meant to be at home in the Realm of Between, though many are seldom aware of this beautiful communion and seldom open to it. Those who do not know the Realm of Between are like a man who dwells in a lovely country but who remains inside a small house with the doors closed and the shades pulled down. That man indeed lives in a beautiful country, but he does not see it and he may not know how to open himself to its beauty. Once that man has explored the beautiful country, however, he will no longer be content to stay always in his closed-up house. Once you have entered the Realm of Between in full awareness, you no longer find it satisfying to remain only in your personal reality and personal consciousness.

The Realm of Between transcends time and space. It is like a vast network of personal relationships and interconnections that stretches from the beginning of time to the end of time, and from one end of the universe to the other. It is the favorite realm of God, for in it the Holy Spirit carries out the work of bringing the world to its completion in fullest consciousness. When this completion happens, we will all live in the Realm of Between, the world of loving relationships.

Appendix

The Realm of Between is accessible to us now. Kything is one way of stepping into it. For those on a spiritual path, the goal is to learn to move into this realm easily and quickly, and to spend more and more time there. Whoever is at home in the flow of this spiritual network functions as easily across the apparent abyss of death as ordinary humans step back and forth across the thresholds of their homes. When you kythe, you learn to become conscious that you are in the Realm of Between, and that you are able to be present to (be in communion with) anyone in that vast network, on either side of death. You and any partner you choose are able to be unconditionally loving and openly present, spirit-to-spirit, to each other.